The ABC's of Dollhouse Finishing

From Kit to Masterpiece

By Barbara Warner

From the publishers of *Nutshell News*

KALMBACH  BOOKS

First printing, 1994. Second printing, 1995.

Library of Congress Cataloging-in-Publication Data
Warner, Barbara.
    The ABC's of Dollhouse finishing : from kit to masterpiece / Barbara Warner.
      p. cm.
      Includes index.
      ISBN 0-89024-192-9

      1. Dollhouses. I. Title.
TT175.3.W37 1994   QBI94-1698

FRONT COVER CREDITS
COACHLIGHT: Scott's Lighting
DOG: Gail Morey
DOOR: Houseworks
DOOR HARDWARE: Realife
LADDER: White Horse Miniatures
PAINT: Builders' Choice
PAINT CAN, ROLLER AND PAN, BRUSH,
    SCREWDRIVER, CAULKING GUN: Pot metal
    miniatures painted by Louise Levitt
SIDING: Midwest

DISCLAIMER
All information is presented in good faith. However, no warranty is given and results are not guaranteed. The Author disclaims any liability for injury resulting from the use of recommended tools and materials.

ACKNOWLEDGMENTS

A special thanks to my husband, Tom, who spent a Sunday painting the moldings for the Twelve Oaks as he watched the football games on TV.

My other helper, Margaret (Maggie) Geen, spent two days helping me wallpaper the Twelve Oaks and paint its windows and doors. For this I am truly grateful.

Special thanks to Robert Bell, Phyllis Tucker, Brian Rehill, Barbara Hoffman, Janet Hermes, Lee Talmadge, Arlene Hines, and Dean Benamy for their advice and aid. It's much appreciated!

CONTENTS

1 WELCOME TO THE WORLD OF DOLLHOUSES

The Colonial interior of the Newport has fireplaces in the main rooms and is lit with candle fixtures.

Come with me and I'll show you how to finish your dollhouse in the most efficient, enduring ways possible. This book offers detailed instructions for exterior and interior decorating of whatever shell or kit you've chosen. If you've not yet bought your kit or shell, read the first two chapters of this book. They'll help you choose the dollhouse you want.

In general, it is better to put the dollhouse together yourself, so you can make changes and do some of the decorating as you go. If you're having someone assemble the shell for you, keep in mind that it's simpler to paint parts before they are assembled. If you want your helper to paint, wire, wallpaper, etc., for you, you can save time by having these steps done as the shell is being constructed. A basic way of finishing a kit is to have your builder prime the walls, paint the ceiling, and wire the house as he or she assembles the main body of the house. Later, when the wallpapering is done, the trims, doors and windows, and staircases will be permanently installed.

Dollhouse kits are generally classified by the design of their construction—they can be pre-cut plywood, tongue-and-groove, or

The Colonial-style
Newport is a totally
enclosed pre-cut
plywood house kit with
front-opening walls.

Top: The interior of the Twelve
Oaks is finished in a contemporary
traditional style. Bottom: The
plantation-style Twelve Oaks is a
pre-cut plywood house kit with an
open-back access to the inside.

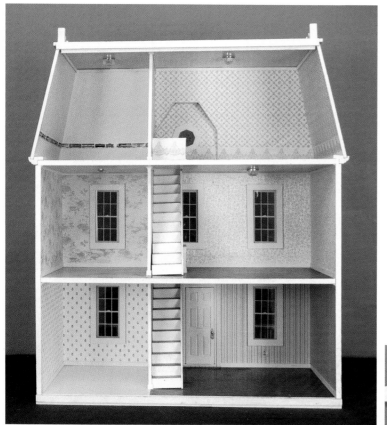

tab-and-slot. Each type meets different needs. The pre-cut plywood house is usually sturdiest. Simpler styles are especially nice for children, as they can withstand being played with. The tongue-and-groove house usually has large rooms and interesting exterior facades. The tab-and-slot house is generally more appealing architecturally. It characteristically has lots of nooks and crannies and gingerbread trim.

The pre-cut plywood house comes with parts cut from ⅜" sheet plywood. Sometimes smaller houses are assembled at the factory and come from the box ready to paint and finish. A house like this is called a shell. More often a house comes as a kit and must be assembled. When the doors,

Casey's house, the pre-cut plywood Cranberry Cove, is decorated with her favorite colors of purple, red, and blue.

windows, and stairs are included, they are often pre-assembled. There may be die-cut sheets of trim in the kit too. Some nationally known kit brands are Real Good Toys, Walmer, Afton Classics, G. E. L. Products, Celerity, and Lawbre.

The dollhouse made of tongue-and-groove panels has bundles of pre-cut pieces that the builder must assemble to make the walls before constructing the house. The pine panels are ¼" thick—milled clapboard on one side, and smooth on the other. The interlocking edges are finished with a groove on one and a tongue on the other. These panels are set into pine corner posts. At one time, parts for the doors and windows were pieces of stripwood that were

The Heritage, a tongue-and-groove house kit, has its exterior colored in a "painted lady" Victorian style. The interior is a series of Christmas workshops.

bundled and pre-cut. Now most of them are die-cut plywood. Die-cut sheets of trim are common in these kits, as are redwood shingles for the roof. Enough wood veneer strips are provided to floor at least one level of the house. Stairs are included and must be assembled. Dura-Craft manufactures this kind of kit.

The tab-and-slot kit comes with sheets of ⅛" plywood that have been stamped (die-cut) with the parts. They must be punched out and assembled to make the house. Doors, windows, and stairs—which must be assembled—and sometimes shingles are included in the kit. Greenleaf manufactures this kind of kit.

Since architectural style is important, too, the sample houses used in the book

illustrate some of the more popular looks. The brick, front-opening house is done in a Colonial or Georgian style. The interior reflects the influence of Adams' architecture on the earlier homes in our country. Many-paned windows, wrought iron lighting, and paneled shutters are reflections of the materials available at that time. With a few adjustments, the house could be turned into a Georgian home in England. This house is made from a pre-cut plywood kit called "Newport."

The plantation house is a Greek Revival style reminiscent of the Federal/Empire era in the United States. Interior decoration leans toward a traditional look. Louvered shutters, classical columns, and windows with larger panes show the influence of

The staircase in the Glencroft is an unusually nice design. It doesn't intrude into the rooms and hides the fireplace breasts.

France on the houses built in this country during the early 1800s. This house, called "Twelve Oaks," is a pre-cut plywood kit, too.

"Casey's dollhouse" is a mansard-roofed house with a porch. It was finished for a child, so the decoration is eclectic and easy to care for. Siding and wiring were added to the kit. The house was made from the "Cranberry Cove" kit. This house has been played with by a six-year-old and a two-year-old, and it has held up very well. The only parts harmed were the lights that could be grabbed and pulled or twisted off.

The "Nutcrackers' Workshop" is Victorian Gothic in style. Because the configuration of the interior is very open, it seemed best as a fantasy house. The Hallmark Nutcracker ornaments inspired a Christmas theme. Each room became a different workroom reflecting the character of the individual nutcrackers. The house is made from a tongue-and-groove kit called "Heritage."

The cottage is a half-timbered Tudor style. It originated in the 1600s and reappears every 100 years or so with innovations of the current times. It was a very popular trend during the 1920s and '30s in both England and the U.S. This sample has an English cottage look and is probably more an English house than an American one. Some clues to this are the use of tile in the kitchen, the gaslight, and the doors opening into the room, rather than against the wall. This house is made from a tab-and-slot kit called "Glencroft."

Use this book in conjunction with the instructions in your dollhouse kit. The chapter headings follow the general order of procedure in assembling and decorating a dollhouse. When special instructions are needed for a certain type of house, they are included at the proper point of construction. Study the book and plan your strategy for completing your miniature abode.

2 PLANNING THE FINISHED PROJECT

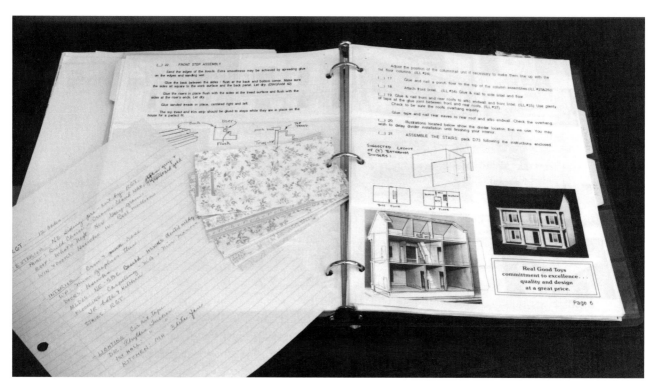

Use a three-ring binder to hold your dollhouse ideas, instructions, and journal.

Since you are embarking on what will be a voyage into Miniature Land, it's best to set your itinerary before you begin. It's not a hard and fast schedule but rather a guide to help you to move forward and not have to backtrack. As with any Grand Tour, it's best to keep a journal. In it you will have your master plan and notes on all the exciting extras you want to add to your project. You may even enjoy keeping entries on cost, anecdotes about your house, and comments on items purchased for it.

In preparing this book, I used a three-ring binder to hold the instructions from my kit. I put my notes on notebook paper, which I also kept in the binder. I punched holes in the installation directions from the flooring packaging and added them also. As I did the wallpapering, I cut 3" x 5" samples from the scraps and put them in a plastic bag taped in the front of the binder. Later, whenever I needed to match carpeting, paint, or furniture, I could take these samples with me to do my shopping.

If you haven't purchased your house or kit yet, there are some things to consider as you are making your choice.

Try to shop where there are made-up examples of the house you're interested in. Then you can examine the size of rooms, see what type of wood it's made of, and learn a little about how it goes together. If you already have some of the furniture you will put in the house, take the pieces with you to try in the sample. This may be an important step if you have some questions as to whether or not the house is suitable.

Examine the wood in the house and decide whether you can handle the construction—or in some cases the customizing—of the kit. Kits with many pieces take longer to finish. That's not a problem if you know about it from the start. Ask the salesperson your construction questions, or if no one is there, read further on into this book. Look for the details you want to know about.

Two criteria are essential in choosing a house, and they are frequently overlooked. One is the attic space and the other is the staircase or staircases. Since a dollhouse is a confined area, every bit of space needs to be usable.

In assessing the attic or upper floor, look for rooms high enough to accommodate what you want to display there. In a house with a peaked roof, the floor-to-peak distance has to be at least 11" if you want to put beds, a chest of drawers, or dolls in the area. If you examine the examples in this book, you will see that the attic in the Nutcrackers' Workshop is very short. It works because portable musical instruments and animals are all that will be in the space.

Houses with mansard roofs have the most space in the upper floor. This style of roof gives the attic almost straight walls and usually a ceiling as high as the ceiling on the lower floors.

Staircases are usually space-wasters and are not particularly pretty. In a child's dollhouse, however, they are a necessity. Children love to move their dolls up and down the steps, so the stairs should be sturdy and should face the open side of the house. In a collector's house, stairs are not as important. They can be inconspicuously hidden behind walls or even just suggested. Some miniature houses are without stairs simply because the owner feels it's more important to use the space for furnishings. When viewing a house like this, you usually don't notice the lack of stairs unless the architecture of the house is more important than the objects that are displayed in it.

If the dollhouse is for a child, look for a kit that features sturdy construction and a minimum of breakable trim. Plan on lighting the house, but use fixtures that mount flush to the ceiling.

After all these considerations, choose the house or kit you like. Any obstacles can be overcome with a little thought and planning, and it's fun to turn those obstacles into ingenious advantages.

After you've purchased your house, daydream about it. If your house is still in the box, dig the directions out of the kit. Read them over and write ideas in pencil on the various pictures. If your dollhouse is already in the shell state, set it in a spot where you will see it frequently. If you have furniture or other pieces you want to use in the house, it helps to put them out where you can see them. Arrange them on a table or shelf or put them in the shell.

If your dollhouse comes to you as an unfinished shell, don't accept delivery if the staircase or staircases, windows, doors, or interior trim have been permanently glued in place. That sounds drastic, but the Voice of Experience speaks. If these items are in place, it will take a lot more effort to finish the walls and floors, and when you are done it will look slipshod. That's not acceptable when it can be prevented.

When you make arrangements to have the shell assembled, tell the builder specifically not to install these items permanently. If he does, have him remove them.

Study your house's exterior and interior architectural features. They can inspire unique use of nooks and crannies. Often they help set the time frame for the house.

Decide if your house is contemporary or historical. If you are going to do a period piece, research the era to make the project as authentic as possible. Keep notes in your notebook, along with sources. Books, magazines, museums, old movies, TV programs about historical places, antiques, and travel are good suppliers of information. Sometimes just researching the architectural style of your house helps you decide the color scheme and location of rooms.

Designate the function of each room. Decide which will be the kitchen, which will be

The upper floors of the Nutcrackers' Workshop demonstrate how to use striped and allover-design wallpaper on angled walls.

the living room, and so on. Dollhouses often do not have enough rooms on one level to be logical. Many houses only have two rooms per floor, so think in a Continental mode. In Europe and any large city where ground level space is at a premium, it is normal to have the living room or reception area on the second floor, along with the master bedroom. Floors above this are used for the bathroom and bedrooms for children and servants. The rooms on the ground level are usually the kitchen and dining room.

If a dollhouse is very small, eliminate rooms that you don't like or are hard to furnish. You can always say that those rooms are in the missing part of the house and that the observer has to imagine them.

Dollhouses tend to have staircases in silly places, so take a careful look at their location in your house. If a staircase interferes with what you want the room to be, consider moving it, reversing it, or even elimi-

nating it. At times the staircase can provide an alcove for a bed, desk, closet, or even a secret corner.

Some dollhouses have rooms, gables, or whole floors that need special attention during construction. L-shaped houses like the Pierce (made by Greenleaf) have rooms in an almost completely enclosed corner. This area will have to be totally decorated before the rest of the house is finished.

When working in gable areas, determine if the alcove needs extra partitions to straighten the walls so that furniture may be placed against them. Actually, every attic area should be examined to see if it would be more usable with the walls squared up.

In some dollhouses the gables are too small to get your hands into them to work. In the Nutcrackers' house it was easier to decorate that space before putting in the third floor. Note that in the middle, the wallpaper was left loose to go around the corner onto the attic partition. This was

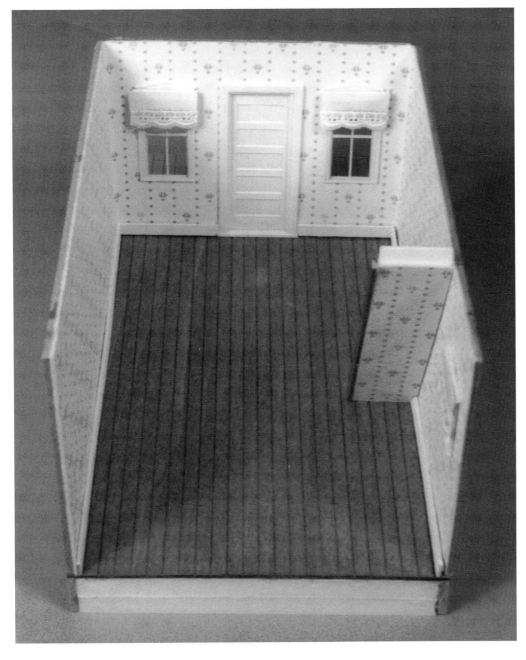

The first floor of this 1/4" scale house is entirely decorated—curtains installed and staircase in place—before the second floor is glued in place.

then finished when the floor and partition were added.

A smaller scale house is simpler to construct if you totally decorate a floor before adding the second floor or roof. This means working from the ground up. Put in the first floor flooring, the partitions, the lighting, wallpaper, windows, doors, moldings, stairs, curtains, and any shelves that will be hung on the wall. In the case of 1/4" scale, glue the furniture in place, too. Then add the next floor or roof.

Architecture, historical period, and furnishings frequently inspire a color scheme for a house. An attractive wallpaper or a fine fabric can set up a whole scheme by suggesting the main color plus all the complements to it. The prettiest color on a paint chart can be the basis of your decorating plan. If the dollhouse is to be a part of the appointments in a full-size room, you may coordinate the small house's color selection with the room.

In another vein, your project could be the reflection of a holiday, a celebration, or a season of the year. Most of these automatically suggest the colors to use. To make the colors more subtle, use shades and tints instead of garish hues. The red and green colors of Christmas, for instance, could be interpreted in burgundy, maroon, cranberry, brick red, and hunter, sage, and sea foam green set off by off white, cream, or pale gold.

When you have a color scheme worked out, plan to paper the interior—even the solid-colored walls. Wallpaper gives a much smoother surface than paint and takes less time to apply. Most dollhouses don't have smoothly surfaced wood in them, which means the wall finish is rough. That may be an advantage in a rustic setting, but generally you don't want a rough wall finish.

When selecting the wallpaper for your dollhouse, coordinate the different designs carefully. A miniature house is different from a real one in that all the rooms are visible at the same time. So it's usually best to have one unifying color in all the rooms.

This window is properly recessed in a brick wall, just as windows are in reality.

Pay attention to the line design in your wallpapers, too. If you select all stripes, small prints, or diagonals, the overall effect can be boring or too busy. Mix the line designs. A stripe style is a good spacer between a print and a geometric. When two prints are next to each other, make one small and the other large or airy. If the colors are compatible, it works. The photo of the Nut-

crackers' Workshop upper floors shows an example of line design contrast.

If your dollhouse has complicated ceiling lines in the attic, try an all-over pattern there. Avoid stripes, plaids, and geometrics. Besides being difficult to match, strong linear patterns tend to be too chopped-up in this scenario. You can, however, use a strong stripe to advantage to emphasize the dormers.

Do wire your house for electricity! Of all the things that have recently become available in miniatures, small lighting fixtures are the most wonderful. It's magical! From a practical point of view, lighting makes it easier to see the collection of furnishings in the house, especially if the rooms are deeper than four inches.

Electric wiring needs to be done before you wallpaper. Plan it now so you have some idea where the hardware will run. If your dollhouse directions have a picture of the interior, you can pencil in the probable positions of the light fixtures.

The easiest wiring system to use is tape wire. Its greatest advantage is that fixtures may be installed anywhere along the tape, even after the house is fully decorated. With conventional round wire your fixture scheme has to be more definite. You must plan how you'll hide the wire—in a groove or under molding—and map that out before you begin assembly.

If you are doing a period piece, you can still use electricity; but have the fixtures be candles, gaslight, or oil lamps. Part of your research will be to determine what type of lighting to use in your project. Books about antiques have a surprising amount of information on the subject.

Decide how you are going to finish the outside of your house. The simplest finish is paint. If you decide later that you would prefer siding, brick, or roofing, you can add it easily. A paint finish is excellent for children's houses. It will take the wear and tear of being played with.

Most dollhouses are designed to be finished with clapboard siding. Several companies produce nice siding sheets that can be added as the shell is put together. Some manufacturers offer pre-cut siding to fit their houses. If your manufacturer offers it, use it.

If you are doing a Tudor timber-framed house, you will want stucco or brick between the exposed timbers. The easiest way to stucco is to mix fine-textured grit into paint and apply that to the wall. Textured wallpaper is another simple way to achieve a stucco look.

Some dollhouse designs lend themselves to being finished with brick. Magic brand "Brik" plaster product is probably the most widely used. If you are going to use a brick finish, you will have to do some customizing of the windows and doors in the kit. They should be recessed in the brick walls, whereas the door and window framing on a sided house lies on top of the clapboard.

The window pictured opposite is on an English dollhouse and is properly recessed. Most English dollhouses are made this way because the majority of real houses there have windows recessed in the walls. Unfortunately, American dollhouse manufacturers do not make a kit specifically meant to look like a brick house. You can only attempt to camouflage the openings as much as possible, as was done on the Newport.

Next, decide what roof treatment to use. Again, paint is the simplest finish. It looks nice with any style of exterior finish and is the most practical for a child's house.

If you want to use a roofing material, several types are available. Asphalt shingles come in rolls and are stapled on the house. Wooden shingles come in rectangle and patterned styles and are individually glued in place. Tile, slate, and corrugated metal roofs are made in plastic sheets.

When your house is done you will want to put it on display. Put it on a sturdy table that can support its weight. You should be able to see a house with an open back from both front and back.

Since it is awkward for most of us to display a dollhouse in the middle of a room, there are a couple of solutions. Put a smaller house or a town house on a turntable. There is one on the market that carries electricity and is easily connected to a transformer. A longer house would totter dangerously on a turntable and is better on a table with casters. Then the whole assembly can be swung out to show the back of the house.

The dollhouse that opens from the front can be pushed against a wall. Small ones even fit conveniently on a shelf. This kind of house usually has a whole front wall that opens like a door on a cupboard.

As you are planning how to display your project, decide if you will want landscaping. If space is available, trees, shrubs, and

The painted roof on Casey's house is a wise choice. Little fingers can't pull off the shingles.

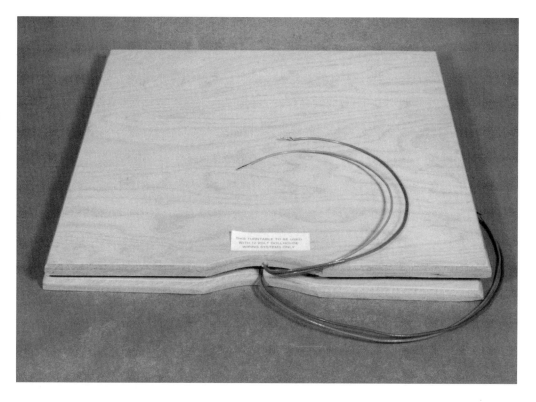

This electrified turntable was used under the Nutcracker's Workshop (Heritage).

flowers will enhance the house. Mount landscaping on a separate base from the table top and set the house on this base. You may fasten the house to the base, but make it detachable for moving. You want to be able to get it through a doorway.

In this planning stage, accumulate most of your supplies before you begin. If you can't get them together all at once, map out your work ahead of time and get supplies as you progress. Write your plans in your notebook, so you have them to refer to.

Take your time in construction and enjoy every aspect of it. Don't push yourself to complete one more area when you are tired. Take a break! Do the more tedious parts when you are fresh. In the long run it will save you time, since you won't have to re-work mistakes made when you were tired.

Some people think building a dollhouse is like decorating a full-size house. It is, sort of, but the dollhouse is more fun because it's your fantasy! Don't skip the next chapter, "Finishing Formulas and Gluing Procedures." It will help you plan your assembly procedures in the chapters that follow.

3 FINISHING FORMULAS AND GLUING TECHNIQUES

FINISHING FORMULAS

Throughout this book you will find instructions to apply primer, paint, stain, clear finish, or a final finish to segments of your dollhouse. Successful, time-saving techniques for doing these tasks are detailed in this chapter. Read this before starting your house so you can choose the simplest ways to finish your kit.

TO PRIME A SURFACE

You'll need the following supplies for priming:

- White-pigmented shellac, such as the one made by Zinsser. Ask for it at a full-service paint store. This brand is also available at Builders' Square, a home building center. In England, there is a "white French polish." If this is French polish with white pigment in it, it can be substituted for white-pigmented shellac. Try it on a scrap of wood. After it's dry, apply acrylic or emulsion paint over it. If it doesn't get gummy or crackle, it's a product comparable to shellac.
- 1½" sash brush with slant-cut bristles. The brush pictured has a shortened handle, so it's easier to use in close quarters.
- 150 to 220 garnet, aluminum oxide, or production sandpaper. Don't use flint paper, as it scratches a surface rather than smoothing it.
- Scrap block of hardwood, such as oak.
- Brown paper bag or cheap paper towels.
- Rag.

Primer is the unsung hero of a finely finished surface. Its purpose is to seal the surface and provide a uniform color over which paint or wallpaper may be applied. In painting, the primer sets up the surface so that only two coats of paint will usually provide a final finish. Under wallpaper, primer provides a sealed, uniform, smooth white surface that won't absorb the wallpaper paste.

White-pigmented shellac has proven to be the best primer for dollhouses. It is white and seals wood or fiberboard against moisture from water-base paint, glue, or wallpaper paste. It brings up and hardens the grain for easy sanding. Its odor is tolerable, and it dries in 15 minutes. It is compatible with acrylics or latex paint. It has a solvent base, denatured alcohol, which helps prevent warping in thinner woods. And finally, it is a true sealant. It is sold to treat water stains and seal sap spots in wood. For clean-up, use denatured alcohol. (In England, it's methylated spirits.) Once the shellac is out of the brush, clean it again with soap and water.

One discovery I made while preparing this book was the existence of white-pigmented shellac in a spray can. It saved a lot of time in priming dollhouse moldings, door and window frames, and staircase parts. More detailed directions for using the spray shellac and making holding jigs are in the chapters on finishing these parts.

White latex or acrylic paint, gesso, and oil-base primer are frequently recommended as primers. They will work, but require more effort to use. White latex or acrylic is water-based, which can cause warping in thinner woods. It also takes 30 days to cure and become waterproof. Gesso is also water based and requires several coats for its "filling" properties to work successfully. It may be used over white-pigmented shellac to make a satiny smooth surface when needed.

Oil-base primer has a noxious odor and takes longer to dry. You also must use mineral spirits or paint thinner to clean your brush—another sickening toxic odor. When using these products, work in a well-ventilated area, as their odors can cause diarrhea and headaches.

APPLYING THE PRIMER

Don't sand the surface before applying the primer. That's usually an unnecessary step. The shellac will harden the surface fibers, making it easier to smooth away the roughness. Use a vacuum cleaner, brush, or rag to remove all dust and debris from the surface to be primed.

Stir the shellac, making sure the pigment is distributed throughout. The pigment has a tendency to settle and may need to be stirred periodically while you're using it.

Apply the shellac with the sash brush. It is a practical size for the broader surfaces and, with its angled bristles, is usable on windows and doors too. The shellac will be dry to the touch within about 20 minutes. After an hour it is usually dry enough to burnish or sand.

When smoothing dollhouse walls or ceilings, rub them with the block of hardwood or a piece of crumpled brown paper from a grocery bag. To smooth siding or shaped moldings, doors, and windows, rub the surface with rough paper towel or the brown paper. Try the methods that don't create sawdust first—less clean-up.

If you use sandpaper, use the rougher grit for coarse-grained wood and finer grit for smoother surfaces. Wrap the sandpaper around the hardwood block to sand flat surfaces. When the surface is smooth, remove the debris for the next step.

TO PAINT A SURFACE

You will need the following:
- Semi-gloss acrylic or latex paint. A quality brand for dollhouses is Builders' Choice, which is the one many miniature shops stock. In England there is a finish, which I think is called "eggshell," that is equivalent to the American finish. Ask at your local paint store for a water-base semi-gloss or satin finish paint. Read the labels and look for soap and water clean-up. That's the key clue as to whether or not it is this kind of paint. The paint pot samples are just right for dollhouse work, but are usually matte finish emulsion paint. This is usable, but should be sealed with clear acrylic satin varnish.

OR
- Matte acrylic or latex paint. Ceramacoat, Accent, and Folk Art are a few of the

brands available at craft stores and some miniatures shops. The color selection is fabulous. The paint comes in 2-ounce plastic bottles, just the right amount for a multi-color finish on a Victorian "painted lady." If you use the matte finish, you will need to apply a coat of acrylic satin varnish as the final coat. It seals the matte surface and makes the finish washable. In England, I used "Humbrol acrylic colour," which comes in 12 ml pots. I also used artist's tube acrylics and thinned them with water and acrylic extender. The clear water-base varnish mentioned above is available at an art supply store.

- 1½"sash brush with slant-cut bristles or ¾" glaze brush (Bought in a ceramic supply shop)
- 220 or 400 sandpaper as necessary
- Block of hardwood, cheap paper towel, or brown paper bag
- Rag

The preferred paint for a dollhouse is a brush-on semigloss or satin finish acrylic. It gives you a nice finish with only two coats of paint. This kind of paint is dry to the touch in 20 minutes to an hour. It takes 30 days to totally cure. Cleanup is with soap and water. Dried paint, in brushes, may be soaked out in denatured alcohol. (In England, it's methylated spirits.) After flaking the old paint from the brush with a stiff toothbrush, give the brush a final wash in soap and water.

Always wash the wet paint out of the brush with soap, either dishwashing liquid or bar bath soap. Rinsing the brush only with water doesn't clean it. The soap will always bring out more pigment from what appears to be a clean brush.

You will quickly learn not to let acrylic paint dry in your brush. It doesn't come out, and the brush will have to be soaked in denatured alcohol. However, if you find you don't want to clean a brush because you will soon use it for another part of the house, you can keep it from drying out by slipping the brush into a plastic bag. Squeeze all the air out and close the bag around the brush handle with a rubber band. If it will be longer than an hour between painting times, you can save the brush longer by

putting it in the freezer. This works with shellac and varnish also.

You may want to use an airbrush to finish the dollhouse. It is especially handy for trims, doors, and windows. When using this tool, take precautions. Work in a well-ventilated area with ample protection to the furnishings around the worktable. Paint particles will be in the air, and they settle everywhere. Since clean-up with this tool is tedious, it's best to plan to do all the pieces that will be the same color simultaneously.

Aerosol can spray paint is another way to paint hard-to-finish pieces like the grid on windows and French doors and spindles for railings. Precautions as mentioned above must be used with this method too. A spray can will send paint particles further afield than the air brush. A spray box can be used to contain some of the dust. However, it's easiest to use the spray paint out of doors on a windless day. Work in an area where colored dots on grass or tree trunks will not cause a problem.

In general, the brush-on paint is simpler to use. It doesn't require as much cleanup time or special preparations to use the tools.

HOW TO PAINT A SURFACE

The surface you are going to paint should already be primed, smoothed, and dust free.

Thoroughly stir the paint. A tongue depressor works well in an 8-ounce can. A coffee stirrer, an ice cream stick, or a paddle-shaped wax working tool is usable in the narrow-necked 2-ounce bottle.

If you're working with paint that comes in a jar or bottle too narrow to put the brush in, pour the paint into an old cream pitcher, gravy boat, or measuring cup—something with a spout lip. The container is wide enough to accommodate the brush, and when you finish with the paint it is easily poured back into the original container.

Use the 1½" brush for most surfaces. Dip the brush about ¼" into the paint. Don't wipe excess paint off on the side of the can. You can pick up foreign bits that mar the finished surface. It's better to barely pick up enough paint and tip the bristles upright to carry the paint to the surface you are painting. Use the ¾" brush when painting things like windows, doors, and balusters.

When the first coat is dry, feel the surface for smoothness. If it's not as nice as you would like, try burnishing it with the block of hardwood or paper towel or brown paper bag. If you're still not satisfied after that treatment, use a 220 or 400 grit sandpaper and lightly sand the surface.

Clean off any dust residue. Apply the second coat. Usually that's all that's needed. Let it dry thoroughly.

NOTE: Matte acrylic needs a final clear finish of water-base varnish.

TO STAIN A SURFACE

You'll need the following:
- Minwax or other brand oil-base stain. In England, "wood dye" is very similar. This has very noxious fumes, so be sure to use it in a well-ventilated area.
- Foam brush or a rag to apply stain.
- Rag to remove excess stain.
- Disposable plastic or rubber gloves to protect your hands from being stained.

Oil-base stain is the best choice for staining floors and woodwork in a dollhouse. It gives better color coverage and doesn't warp thin wood, as water-base does. Cleanup is with mineral spirits, paint thinner, or turpentine. (In England, it's "white spirits.") Remember to work in a well-ventilated area

because of noxious fumes. The best way to avoid the fumes is to use a disposable applicator, either a rag or a foam brush. Take it out of the work area immediately so the odor doesn't get a chance to contaminate your workspace.

To apply the stain, use the rag when you need control over the amount of stain applied and the brush when it's necessary to saturate the surface. When you are staining a paper-backed flooring, use the rag. You don't want the stain to loosen the wood from the backing.

HOW TO STAIN A SURFACE

Smooth the surface to be stained with sandpaper. As the final smoothing step, burnish the area with a piece of wood, paper towel, or brown paper bag. It should be silky to the touch. Remove all sawdust with a vacuum, rag, or brush.

Shake the can of stain vigorously before opening. Have it mechanically shaken at the paint store where you purchase it, if possible. When you open the can, stir the paint to make sure any sediment in the bottom of the can is thoroughly mixed in. Dark stains like walnut tend to settle, whereas light stains like golden oak have little residue.

Don the plastic gloves. Using the appropriate applicator, wipe on the stain by stroking it on the length of the board. Usually one swipe does it. Normally you have time to apply all the stain to a floor or stain several pieces of woodwork before you must wipe off the excess stain. Use a second rag to wipe away the excess. If you want a darker color, apply a second coat and don't wipe away so much color. The hue you see when the stain is wet is usually close to the color it will be when you give the piece its final clear finish.

Let the stain dry. It usually takes several hours. When it's thoroughly dry, burnish the surface with a rag, paper towel, or wood block. It's now ready for a final clear finish.

TO FINISH A SURFACE WITH CLEAR SHELLAC

You'll need the following:
- Clear shellac with a current shelf life date. (Shellac does get old and won't dry properly.) In England, it is called clear

or plain French polish. So-called button polish has a darkening agent added to it.

- Clear or colored paste wax, depending on the color of the surface you are finishing.
- Soft, clean rags like old T-shirts or cloth diapers.

Occasionally when finishing a dollhouse you will use unstained wood for the floor. The raw color, like mahogany or walnut, is so pretty it is a crime to cover it. This type of floor can be beautifully finished with clear shellac.

Clear shellac may also be used as a sealing coat on a stained surface. While preparing floors for this book, I frequently discovered that I needed only one coat of water-base varnish after sealing the surface with clear shellac.

In England shellac, or French polish, comes in a plastic bottle with a narrow neck. This is sensible, since the shellac is best applied by rag and rubbed into the wood with a circular motion. You may want to pour your can of shellac into a clean plastic bottle or an empty denatured alcohol can. Denatured alcohol is the solvent for shellac. In England, it's methylated spirits.

HOW TO APPLY SHELLAC

The surface you are covering should be clean and silky smooth to the touch. Use the techniques described above for burnishing or sanding, and vacuum away the dust. Work with a good light positioned slightly to the side of your working area. You want to be able to see the light bounce off the wet surface so you know you are covering the entire area with the clear finish.

Make a pad of a clean, soft rag, pour some shellac on it, and rub it into the surface of the wood using a circular motion.

You will find it dries almost instantly. Apply at least two coats. You may find that three to five coats is best. This is a very thin layered finish. When you can see a sheen on the surface after it's dry, it is right.

Let the surface dry thoroughly. As a final coat, apply paste wax with a soft rag. Burnish this with a second clean, soft rag. This finish is perfect for parquet flooring, as the paste wax tends to fill gaps and make the surface smooth.

When using the clear shellac as a sealing coat under varnish, use a brush to apply it. When it is dry, apply the varnish and finally paste wax.

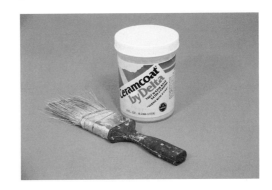

TO APPLY A CLEAR FINISH TO A STAINED OR PAINTED SURFACE

You'll need the following:

- Ceramcoat Water Base Satin Varnish. In England, I used a water base varnish from the art supply store. I believe the brand was Liquitex.
- 1½" sash brush with slant-cut bristles.

Be sure the previous coat of stain, shellac, or paint is thoroughly dry. The surface should be smooth to the touch.

Use a paint stirrer or tongue depressor to stir the varnish thoroughly, as the sediment is the ingredient that gives the satin finish. Try not to have bubbles form in the liquid. Keep the tip of the stirrer submerged and move it from the bottom up. It's a lot like folding egg whites into cake batter. Keep stirring gently until the sediment seems suspended in the liquid. You're now ready to apply the varnish.

Have good light shining at an angle from the side of your work area so you can see when the surface you are varnishing is completely covered.

Dip your brush ¼" into the varnish.

Don't tap it on the side of the can and pick up dried bits. Tilt the bristles upright to carry the varnish to the surface. Flow the varnish onto the surface to be coated. Apply a thin coat. When this coat is dry, check for smoothness. If all is okay, apply a second thin coat. If the surface is rough, burnish it with a rag or paper towel before applying the second coat.

If you are applying this clear finish over stain, you may want to give it a final finish of paste wax.

GLUING TECHNIQUES

There are four indispensable glues for putting together a dollhouse. They are Tacky, Quick Grab, carpenter's or woodworker's glue, and cyanoacrylate gel, or Super Glue in gel form. Listed below are the various glues, their properties, uses, solvents, and techniques for applying them.

One principle holds true for all the glues. The strongest bond will always be to adhere bare element to bare element without an interfering coating like paint. If there is a strain on a bond between painted surfaces, the paint will always give way before the glue does.

TACKY GLUE
(Solvent: Denatured Alcohol)

This is the workhorse of dollhouse construction. Do use Aleene's Original "Tacky" Glue made by Artis, Inc. It is an all purpose white glue that dries clear. It doesn't yellow and has good tack. It may be used on fabric, plastic sheet products, Styrofoam, wood, and other materials.

Use Tacky for wooden shingles, plastic sheet tile, and applying trims, doors, and windows. This glue is good for a strong bond between unlike surfaces such as plastic sheet tile and wood. It sets up quickly, yet allows time for positioning surfaces to be joined.

This glue is water-based and is similar to acrylic paint. It may be thinned with water. When it's thoroughly dry it cannot be dissolved in water, although it will turn milky-colored. Its solvent is denatured alcohol.

If you make a mistake when gluing with Tacky, it is possible to break the bond. Use a small paint brush to drop some denatured alcohol onto the joint. Let it sit for two or three minutes and then gently wiggle the bond. It will usually come apart. If at first it doesn't, apply more denatured alcohol.

Most of the time when you are applying Tacky you will run a bead of glue down a narrow edge of wood. Since the glue grabs immediately when there's a thin layer, it's logical to run your finger down the line to spread the glue. To keep the job from becoming messy, keep a damp rag by your working hand and wipe your finger on it before placing the glue-covered piece in its place. Because this kind of gluing is common in dollhouse construction, you will probably want to keep glue in a Monojet syringe. It lays a thin bead of glue, so necessary when installing moldings.

Monojet syringes tend to drip for many people. They won't if you understand the physics of the tool. The culprit is the air bubble that frequently gets in the glue when you fill the tube. Remove the plunger and squeeze enough Tacky into it to fill the tube one-third full. Place the plunger back in the end of the tube and turn the whole thing so the nozzle is upright. Let the glue run toward the plunger until the air is all on top. Gently push the plunger in the tube, nozzle upright, until all the air is out and the glue is in the nozzle all the way to the opening.

To keep the glue from drying out, cap the nozzle with a knitting needle stitch guard. This is an accessory knitters use to cap the points of their needles when the knitting is laid aside. It can be found anywhere knitting needles are sold.

In England, Tacky glue is available from Jennifer's of Walsall. There is also a Tacky glue sold through needlework and haberdashery shops. The word "tacky" or "tack" is in the title of the glue. It is distributed by one of the needlework suppliers. It comes in the same gold bottle as Aleene's Tacky. I've used it and it seems to be very close to the American product.

CARPENTER'S GLUE
(Solvent: White Vinegar)

This glue is superior for joining wood. The bond will be stronger than wood, which means that the wood will give before the glue will. Use carpenter's glue when constructing all house bodies. It's especially helpful when joining thin plywood pieces.

It is an aliphatic resin, yellow in color, wet or dry. No brand seems to have any superior qualities. The solvent is white vinegar. Carpenter's glue has a similar consistency to Tacky, although it sets up a little more slowly. When applying it, use the same methods as with the Tacky. When possible, clamp the joints with masking tape, bull clips, C-clamps, rubber bands, or snap clothespins. In some instances you will want to weight the joint by placing waxed paper over the project and putting books or heavy canned goods on top.

QUICK GRAB
(Solvent: Rubber Cement Thinner)

3C's Quick Grab is a solvent-based glue. Use it to adhere siding to dollhouses and metal light fixtures to ceilings and walls. This is the glue to use any time you need one that will not cause warping. Because it is solvent-based, it will melt or damage Styrofoam and plastic sheet products.

This glue sets up quickly. When applying it, run a bead of glue along one surface. Spread the glue out by pressing together the two parts to be joined. Open the joint slightly for a few seconds to help activate the bonding. Press the pieces together again and they will hold permanently.

If you make a mistake, use rubber cement thinner (available from a graphic arts store) to break the bond. Apply the thinner with a paintbrush, saturating the bond. Give it a couple of minutes to work and gently pry the joint apart. Since this glue holds so well, it's best to work with the attitude that it will hold forever.

In England, I found UHU Strong Clear Adhesive to be very similar to Quick Grab. It comes in a yellow tube. In testing it for this book, I found it takes longer to set up but seems to hold just as well as the Quick Grab. It has a stronger noxious odor, so always use it in a well-ventilated area.

SUPER GLUE
(Solvent: nail polish remover or "Debonder")

In dollhouse construction, Super Glue, chemically named cyanoacrylate, is usually used in conjunction with Tacky. Super Glue comes in two formulas, a gel and a thin, watery liquid. The gel is a gap filler and preferred when using with Tacky. The thin variety is good for bonding closely matched surfaces. All brands seem to have the same properties.

The solvent for Super Glue is Debonder or nail polish remover. (In England, it's nail varnish remover.) Always have the solvent within reach when working with this glue. It is simple to glue your fingers together, and they don't come apart. Teach yourself safe gluing methods when you work with Super Glue and you won't have problems.

Super Glue has some unique properties. A thick glob of it stays wet for a long while, yet a thin coat sticks instantly. This means it's possible to put out a puddle of it and work from that, using a corsage pin or toothpick to apply the glue. If you get some of it on your finger you can immediately wipe it off on a damp rag and your finger will not stick to your work. "Kick Starter" will quicken the bonding action, and so does spit. Don't lick your finger to remove glue—your finger will stick to your tongue! Super Glue makes a strong but brittle bond. It can't be pulled apart, yet if knocked the right way, especially in light fixtures, the bond often snaps.

Use the Tacky/Super Glue combination for moldings and light fixtures. In some instances, use it in place of Quick Grab. To apply it to a part, dot the surface first with

Tacky glue, and then put the Super Glue in between the Tacky dots. Press the piece to the second surface to spread the glue and make the bond. This makes a strong yet "giving" bond.

Tubes of Super Glue tend to drip when in use. An empty 35mm film canister is a good holder for the glue. Keep the open tube upright in the canister; use the lid as a place to put out your puddle of glue. If you tend to knock things over on the work area, fasten the canister to a scrap piece of wood.

4 WORK SPACE AND PREPWORK

The Heritage kit is in the process of being assembled in my workroom. Notice the walls under construction on freezer wrap.

Your work space

No matter what style kit you put together, you will need a work space. The ideal is a flat surface at about table or counter height, where you can leave your work-in-progress to dry. You'll need an area big enough to lay out the house's foundation. Ideally, it's an area where you can lay out all the main pieces of the house at one time. Whatever surface you use,

though, always cover it with waxed paper or plastic-coated freezer wrap to protect the work table surface from paint, glue, and scratches. Then, when it's necessary to move wet parts, you just pick up the paper, like a tray, and move all to a different place. Pieces painted or glued on either kind of paper are easily loosened if they stick.

Look for a well-lighted place to work in. Daylight is the best, and if you have a space in a sun porch or a room with north-facing windows, that is a heavenly place to work.

Most of us aren't that lucky, so we have to provide lighting. Basic overhead light is necessary. You will also need an adjustable light that can be beamed into awkward corners. A flexible neck desk lamp, an adjustable arm draftsman's or needlework light, or a flashlight will do the trick.

Another very important consideration is ventilation. For most of the work you do on a dollhouse, normal room ventilation is fine. But if you are sanding, sawing, painting with anything you can smell, or gluing with some solvent cements, you are breathing noxious fumes. Use an exhaust fan, open a window, or use a vacuum system that removes the pollution. Always read cans for warnings. Dispose of paint rags immediately in the proper manner.

One extra that makes working on a dollhouse easier is a turntable. As you work you will constantly want to turn the house just a bit to get better light or to reach into a corner. With a turntable, it's a matter of seconds to get it to the new position.

Wooden turntables with ball-bearing hardware are available at miniature shops. Turntable hardware may be purchased at a building center and will require that a "table" be added. Plastic turntables are available in the housewares section of discount and department stores. Use what is appropriate for you—the lighter weight ones for small houses and the sturdier ones for big houses. In preparing this book, the only house I did not make on a turntable was the Twelve Oaks. It was constructed on a table that itself is on casters.

SORT OUT THE BITS

The first thing to do when you open the kit box is locate the directions and schematic drawings or inventory lists. Put them in a three-ring binder. Use a paper punch to put holes in the edges of the pages so that they will turn easily and lie flat when the directions are open.

Using the drawings or lists to guide you, identify the parts and label them. Mark the pieces with pencil, giving them names and kit numbers. If you find it hard to read the pencil markings, use self-stick labels. Never use ball-point or marker pens on wood. That kind of ink stains the wood and bleeds through paint and wallpaper.

If you are assembling a kit that contains die-cut plywood, you will note that the pieces are stamped into sheets of plywood but not cut out. Label all the pieces and remove them from the sheets only when the directions call for the different parts.

At this point, go through the kit's list of components and check them off as you find the pieces. This is an extremely important step. If pieces are missing or broken in your box, phone or write the manufacturer and they will send you a replacement. The manufacturer's address and phone number are usually on the instruction sheet.

Now sort the parts. Find all the pieces of the basic shell and separate them. This includes walls, foundation, floors, room partitions, and roofs. If there are gables, dormers, or bays with multiple pieces, make separate stacks for each segment.

As to the rest of the components, like porches, staircases, and exterior trim, sort and store them in plastic bags or shoe boxes and set them aside for now.

WORKING WITH DIE-CUT PLYWOOD

Many dollhouse manufacturers use die-cut plywood for parts in their kits. It is usually ⅛" luaun mahogany. This is not the best wood to work with, but if you understand some of its idiosyncrasies, you can deal with it successfully.

Because of its thinness, seal both sides of the wood to prevent warping. It's easiest to do this while the pieces are still in the sheets. Determine which pieces need what coating and whether one or both sides should be done. Sides that are entirely glued to another piece of wood usually don't need a coating. Use white-pigmented or clear shellac or stain for this step. When the coating is dry, smooth the surface by rubbing it with a brown paper bag.

Identify and label all the pieces before removing them from the sheets. Use pencil to mark the wood; as mentioned before, pen or marker ink will bleed through subsequent coats of stain or paint. If you use self-stick labels, put them in an inconspicuous place, since they tend to leave a gummy residue that will interfere with some finishes.

Leave the pieces in the sheets until the directions tell you to use them. Punch the designated pieces out by pushing them gently through the sheet. If there's resistance because the cut is not through or because the grain on the back side goes against the scoring, score along the cut line with a craft knife until the piece is free.

You can sometimes punch slots in the center of parts with your thumb if you work from the back side. Work carefully to minimize splintering. Depending on the brand of kit, you may have to enlarge the slots with a rasp or fingernail file.

Two kinds of fingernail files are useful in working on small areas of the dollhouse kit. One is the heavy-duty emery board style used on artificial nails. The other kind is metal with diamond, sapphire, or jewel grit. This one usually lasts longer.

Once punched out, the edges on pieces are usually rough and slightly slanted. Don't zealously sand them to square them up! You will quickly change the shape of the piece and it won't fit properly. Sometimes it's necessary to glue large splinters back in place. Do so immediately with carpenter's glue.

Carpenter's glue is the best kind to use for bonding die-cut plywood pieces together. Many times the narrow edge of a piece is the only contact to an adjacent part. Since the edge is somewhat porous, coat it with carpenter's glue and smear the glue into the edge. Let it dry or set up and then apply a second coat to use for the bonding.

I gave this kind of wood a stained finish for the half-timbered cottage in this book. I had to stain the edges around doors and windows too. Since they were rough and absorbent, I used clear shellac before applying the stain and smoothed the edge with a wood block. I then used matching paste wood filler and applied a clear finish. Edges that I had sanded or carved down to fit an opening were smooth enough to require only the usual method for a stained finish.

A FINAL FINISH FOR THE FLOORS (OPTIONAL)

If you decided when you were planning your dollhouse to finish the floor by staining the wood, now is the time to do it. If you're not using this floor finish, move on to the next heading. This treatment is recommended only for houses with plywood floors. Always stain and varnish before painting. Paint can be wiped off a varnished surface, but stain will not cover paint. Give the floors a final finish following the suggestions in Chapter 3.

The simplest way to do the floors is to stain and varnish all of them, even the kitchen and bath areas. This is a practical finish for a house that will be played with by a child.

You may want to score the floor in a floorboard pattern before staining and varnishing. Using a ruler, mark out the appropriate increments, ¼", ⅜", or ½". A smaller width is used in public rooms, larger in utilitarian ones. Use a T-square to keep the lines even as you mark the scribing with a hard lead, fine point pencil.

Another fairly simple finish is to paint the kitchen and bath areas in colors that coordinate with the rooms' wallpapers. Stain and varnish the rest of the floors.

One way to dress up a painted floor is to border it with strips of striped wallpaper. A printed wallpaper border is another suggestion. Apply the wallpaper trim after the floor is painted. To make it look like a vinyl or a stenciled floor, coat it all with several coats of clear varnish.

PRIME AND PAINT THE SHELL

Before priming the shell, do a dry run with the main pieces. Use masking tape to hold it together. Try getting your hands into the tight places. Map out a strategy for the troublesome areas.

Label the interior walls. This is especially important if you have irregular walls. When you lay the pieces out to prime them, they have a devilish propensity for reversing,

and you end up priming the wrong side.

Dismantle the shell. Lay out the walls and ceilings on your work table, which should be covered with freezer wrap. Make sure you have the right surfaces up. Prime the inside walls and the ceiling sides of the floor-ceiling pieces.

The exterior walls have to be primed if any water-based product will be used on them. That means Tacky, carpenter's glue, wallpaper paste, acrylic paint, stucco, Magic Brik, or any similar product. It's not necessary to prime them if a solvent-based covering, like Quick Grab, will be used. Dollhouses with walls thinner than ¼" plywood should be primed on both sides to prevent warping, regardless.

Paint the ceilings with two or three coats of satin or semi-gloss white acrylic paint. That's a standard finish. If you're giving the ceilings a special treatment, apply it now if you can. Wallpapered ceilings are usually done after the main shell is assembled and the room partitions are in place.

SPECIAL INSTRUCTIONS

This section is for tongue-and-groove kit builders. (If you are assembling a plywood

In Casey's house the kit floor was painted on the left side (the kitchen) and stained and varnished on the right side (the living room).

The row of wood at left is being lined up to make a wall. The right-hand row has been glued together.

or die-cut kit, skip these directions and go to the next heading.) Before you can assemble the shell of your house, you must construct the walls.

Using your kit directions to guide you, gather the appropriate strips of wall wood for each panel. Wipe sawdust and debris off the pieces. Small splintering along cut edges is not important. They will be encased in edge trims and other framing as the building continues.

Lay the strips out on your work table as the directions indicate. Check each strip to be sure it fits into its neighbor correctly.

Assemble each wall panel without glue. Use a T-square or similar tool to make the walls true. When all looks right, glue the walls together with carpenter's glue. Wipe off overflows of glue. Use a rubber-tipped wipe-out tool to remove glue cleanly from crevices. Let the walls dry for 24 hours, flat side down against the table top. Flip them over and let them dry another 24 hours.

The wipe-out tool is a tole painter's aid. (Tole is decorative painting on metal, used for objects like lamps, trays, and boxes.) It's Kemper tool #WOT and is literally used to wipe out paint as a technique. It's a super clean-up tool for glue, as its fine tip gets into tight corners easily. Dried-on glues are easily peeled off its rubber-tipped surface.

While these wall panels are still flat on the table, prime the inside walls and prime and paint the outside ones. The coats of paint help to reinforce the glued seams.

In many kits of this type, a gable wall or two must be shingled and attached to the top of the previously-made wall panel. Your kit directions will give you good instructions for completing this unit.

In addition, when you coat the wall panels with primer and paint, keep the top edge free of finish. You will eventually glue the gables to the top of the wall along this edge.

5 ASSEMBLING THE BODY OF THE HOUSE

At this stage of construction, each type of house needs a different set of directions. Construct the main body of the house, but do not attach the roof until after you've finished the exterior walls.

PRE-CUT PLYWOOD HOUSE

This house is usually a glorified box. The side walls must first be attached to the top, bottom, and middle floors. Then the front or back wall is attached to this frame, squaring up the assembly. The whole unit is glued and nailed to the foundation, which has been constructed separately. Construction is sturdier if brads or panel nails are used along with carpenter's glue.

Before assembling anything, try all the doors and windows in their respective openings, interior and exterior. Square the openings for staircases and doors and windows when necessary. Use the saw from your hobby miter box or a utility knife to cut out the bulk of the waste. Finish the corners with a square rasp.

I found that squaring the doors and windows was necessary when constructing the Twelve Oaks. With the Newport only the stairwells needed squaring. The window and door openings were oversized, and squaring out the corners made the openings too big.

Try doors and windows in every opening. Sometimes, as in the Twelve Oaks, one doorway will be too small. It's a nuisance to correct this fault after the house is built.

I added French doors into the center rooms on the lower floor. I cut the openings for the French doors before installing the partitions.

In the Twelve Oaks, note that I flipped the second and third floor-and-ceiling pieces, so the staircase ended up on the left side of the hall instead of the right. It didn't make any difference in the construction of the stairs, as they are reversible. I flipped the piece to make the smoother side of the wood, which is easier to finish, the ceiling surface. This arrangement also gives a fuller view of the front doors.

Next, drill nail holes on the front and sides of the house according to your kit directions. Support the area to be drilled on a scrap piece of wood or an old phone book, catalogue, or magazine. Use a drill bit a little smaller than the diameter of the nail you will be using. One-inch paneling nails are ideal, since they have a screw groove in the shank that holds nicely in the wood.

The trickiest part of putting this type of house together is getting the first two boards together. You need either a bench stop or an extra pair of hands to help hold boards upright.

To make a bench stop, use a 2 x 4 scrap of wood that is longer than the side of the house, and two C-clamps. In the case of the house in this book, I substituted the bundle of foundation boards for the 2 x 4.

The far wall in the photo is the one being installed. This structure is the main body of the house.

Clamp it to the end of your work table.

First, set one side wall on edge, with the exterior side against the bench stop. Tape the middle floor to the middle of the side wall. Do the same with the bottom floor. Spread carpenter's glue on the edge of both floors and fit the second side wall in place, making sure the wall is square to the floors and the top side edges are flush. Hammer nails through the wall into the two floors. Turn the assembly around so the just-attached side wall is against the bench stop. Pull the tape off the "holding side," glue to the edge of the floors, and attach the second side the same way as the first. Do the same with the remaining top floor.

On the Twelve Oaks, there were grooves in the side walls for the floors, so placing the middle one was easy. On the Newport, everything was measured out and marked on the trial run.

Now attach the front wall (back wall of a front-opening house) to the body of the house. Spread glue on the sides and bottom edges of the body. Put the front wall in place, making the bottom and one side edge flush with the body.

Nail these two edges in place, thereby squaring the house. Nail the third side to the body. At this point, the third side may overhang the body of the house. If this is true, plane or sand the overhang until it is flush.

The Twelve Oaks sample has attic sidewalls and an attic knee wall. Attach them according to the directions in the kit.

The same kit also has side extensions. They use a slightly different construction method, since each has only one side wall. Prime the inside surfaces with white-pigmented shellac and give the ceiling a final finish of white paint—just as you did with the house. Drill the nail holes for attaching the base and the upper floor in the front and side pieces. Use the extension back wall to mark the upper floor position in preparation for drilling the nail holes.

Attach a C-clamp to the side back edge of the upper floor. Tape this to the side wall. Glue and nail the front to the side wall. With the aid of this floor, glue and nail the base floor to the front and side walls. Now do the same with the upper floor. Attach the extensions to the house, following the directions given in the kit.

Now the house is ready for the exterior finish. Countersink the nailheads that show on the open side of the house. Mask the

The C-clamp attached to the side edge of the floor acts as a stand to hold the floor upright during construction.

wall panels according to the directions in Chapter 4. Construct the base and finish the base walls. Lay the wood strip floor. Attach the wall panels to the base. Run the primary wiring. Insert the floors. Since the exterior walls were painted when the wall panels were made, install the front roof. Leave the back roof off until after the attic is wired, wallpapered, and trimmed with molding. Follow the instructions in other chapters of this book for the brickwork, wood strip floors, wiring, and wallpaper.

After completing the foundation as directed, flip the base upside down and reinforce the corners and seams where floor meets base side walls. I used ½" x ¾" stripwood in the example. It's available at any local building center that carries wood for home remodeling.

A fine point of house construction should be noted here. The base of this kit has a brick finish. A trim board is added at the top of the base wall. It must be under the edge of the porch floor. A porch floor is always laid with the boards running from the house to the edge of the porch. This

open side edges of the floors with masking tape. Give the open side edges of the house body and the foundation a final finish—here, with white paint. On the front-opening Newport, the room edges were painted white, but the foundation was painted Cape Cod blue to coordinate with the exterior finish. You're ready to apply the exterior finish following the instructions in Chapter 6.

TONGUE-AND-GROOVE HOUSE

The general procedure with this type of construction is as follows: Assemble the

The small area of interior flooring on the porch at the doorway and the space around the posts are eventually covered with moldings.

allows the rain to run off the porch, so that it won't rot the flooring and trim. The directions for the house being constructed for this book shows the flooring all going in the same direction on the base. Since the strips on the porch floor should go crosswise to the main floor, some modifications were made. The wall panels were taped together and placed in position on the base. A pattern was drawn on the base showing where the porch walls are. The walls were removed and the floor was laid following the directions in Chapter 9 for stripwood floors.

In this style kit, the floors rest on ¼" square molding at the ceiling seam. Give the moldings a final finish before installing them. Leave the sides to be glued free of paint. Follow the kit instructions for location. However, do not install the molding along the baseboard seam until after wallpapering. It's always easier to paint these moldings before installing them. Leave the side to be glued free of paint.

Because of the design of this house, it was easier to wallpaper the first floor walls be-fore the second floor was added and before any roof was on.

The wiring went up the wall with the staircase. The tape wire was not cut off the roll until the front roof was in place and the last of the wiring run was made.

The opening in the third floor was moved so that the ladder comes down in the same room where the staircase comes up. Now the wall space in the second floor center room can be used for a stove.

This sample house was painted, bricked, floored, and papered as it was constructed. It wasn't necessary to have the whole house together and wired before doing these finishing procedures.

TAB-AND-SLOT HOUSE

In these kits, the base is often an integrated part of the walls. The partitions on each floor tend to be above each other and usually joined. Hence, the partition has a slot that the floor slides into and the partition becomes a reinforcing feature of the house construction.

The clips are holding the square moldings in place till dry. The next step is to wallpaper the first floor walls.

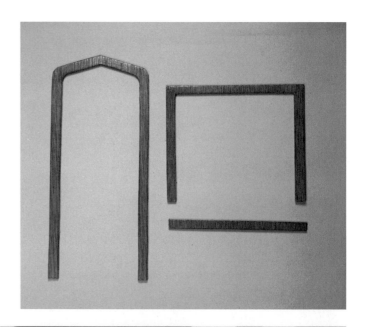

These are the pre-shaped moldings that must be fitted to the door and window openings in the tab-and-slot kit.

This is how the decorated staircase area looks before the side wall is in place.

The Ston finish has been added to the fireplace parts. After being washed with thinned black paint, they will look used.

Before assembling anything in this kit, fit all the doors and windows and make the necessary adjustments while the walls are flat. What's particularly crucial is to fit the interior door and window moldings, as they are pre-shaped, not cut-to-fit trim moldings. Apply a final finish to the edges of the door, fireplace openings, railings, and beams. It's always best to glue the doors and windows permanently in place in a die-cut plywood wall, since hinges are difficult to install and the wood does not hold them well. Just prep the doors and windows at this time. Do not install them. Wait until after the house is papered and painted.

Following the kit directions, assemble the base and walls to the point where the staircase and fireplace exterior walls are ready to be put in place. Glue reinforcing blocks of wood in the base to make it sturdier. Give the open edges a final finish too. They need some spackling paste to fill in holes. Then prime and paint.

Before putting the outside wall on the staircase area, paper the interior wall and lay the carpet on the steps. Install the house wiring too, since it should be accessible for the fireplaces. This is one of those tight areas that is easier to finish before the house body is complete.

In the fireplace areas, apply MagicSton to the fireplace walls and install the "fire" before closing the area with the outside chimney wall.

Because the roof pieces extend into the first floor area, prime and assemble the walls and front roof before wallpapering.

FIREPLACES AND CHIMNEY BREASTS

If you are adding fireplaces to any of the rooms in your kit, give a few moments of thought to their location and how you will accommodate the firebox in or on the wall. Fireplaces were an integral part of decorating the Newport kit. Since they weren't part of the kit, but were purchased separately, they needed chimney breasts to make them look realistic. The chimney breasts had to be added to the house when the body of the house was complete but before partitions were installed.

Two types of chimney breast additions are shown. The first is the fireplace surround with a protruding firebox that must go either into a hole in the wall or a chimney breast that juts out into the room. The second kind is the big kitchen fireplace; it needs a chimney breast on top of the unit to give the allusion that the inside top of the

The fireplaces on the left have floor-to-ceiling chimney breasts. The breasts of the ones on the right rest on the fireplace mantels.

fireplace is open to a chimney. The painted wood fireplace also has a chimney breast added to the top to give a realistic look.

When a fireplace is on the center wall in the room, it must be realistic-looking. Perspective will not hide any defects. When you position the fireplace on a side wall you can sometimes just add the fireplace to the room, paint the wall black where the fireplace opening touches the wall, and say the chimney is in the wall.

Another part of the fireplace that has to be planned is the hearth. In the Newport three of the hearths were inlaid in the flooring. The fourth fireplace unit has a decorative edge on the hearth that would be difficult to inlay, so it was installed on top. The fireplaces in the Glencroft are raised hearths. They had to be finished with MagicSton while the house body was constructed.

If you are adding a fireplace with a firebox to a house, you will have to cut a hole

in the wall of the kit or make a chimney breast. If you cut a hole in the wall, do it before assembling the house body. When you do the dry run, figure out where the hole should be and mark it to be cut before priming the wall.

If you want to use a chimney breast, you have to measure and cut it when you have the house body together and can ascertain where and if it will fit in the room or rooms. In the Newport, the fireplaces in the two left-hand rooms were a tight fit. The doorways are very close to the back wall. When the interior doors were tried in the openings, the door hit the fireplace. To correct the problem, the doors were re-hinged on the other side so they opened into the room, easily clearing the fireplace surround.

Having made chimney breasts in several different ways, I've found that the easiest method is to use a solid piece of wood. In the Newport, 1" x 6" pine boards were cut to fit. Those boards actually measure $\frac{3}{4}$" x $5\frac{3}{4}$". The $\frac{3}{4}$" thickness was just the right depth. Measure the height of the room and subtract $\frac{1}{8}$" from the number to allow for flooring and fitting ease. Trim the board to that height on a scroll saw. Also cut the opening for the firebox, plus $\frac{1}{8}$" for fitting ease. You can use a hand saw for these cuts and a coping saw for the firebox opening.

Cut the chimney breasts that fit on top of the fireplaces to the width of the fireplace and the height between mantel and ceiling less $\frac{1}{16}$".

Set the fireplaces and chimney breasts aside for now. When you install the flooring, install the hearths too. Usually you inlay the hearth in the flooring. The exception is a hearth that is placed on top of the flooring, like the example with the decorative edge.

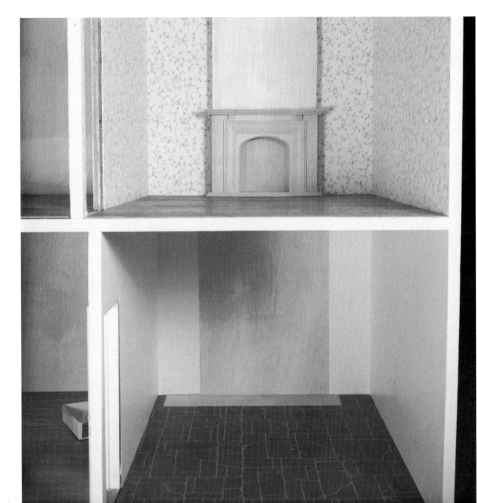

When it's time to wallpaper the room, you may find that you can do it as the Newport was done. One sheet of wallpaper covered each side of the room and ended in the space behind the chimney breast. The chimney breast was papered and glued in place covering the side wallpaper ends.

On a side wall fireplace, it's better to glue the chimney breast in place, then wallpaper over it as part of the side wall. Otherwise, the seam shows where you papered only the chimney breast.

The lower room shows an inlaid hearth in the floor. the wallpaper ends on the back wall, where it will be covered by the fireplace unit.

6 FINISHING EXTERIOR WALLS

The simplest way to finish the outside walls of a dollhouse is with acrylic semi-gloss paint. Countersink any nailheads showing from construction and fill the holes with spackling paste or wood filler, filling in any other imperfections as well while you're at it. Prime the walls with white-pigmented shellac. Smooth the walls and apply two coats of acrylic paint as a final finish. If the wood is somewhat coarse, you may want to use three coats.

If you want a more realistic look, clapboard siding, brick, stone, and stucco products are readily available at your local miniature shop.

CLAPBOARD SIDING

Several companies make clapboard siding. The most widely distributed are Northeastern, Midwest, and Houseworks. All of the pieces are about 3" wide and 24" or 36" long. The clapboard pattern can be ⅛", ¼", ⅜", or ½". When buying siding for your house, be sure to note the clapboard width and which brand you are buying. Make sure all pieces match, since there is enough variance between brands to make them incompatible.

When you select your siding, choose a brand with a notched edge that will overlap the preceding board. This detail hides seams, giving a more uniform look to the finished house.

If your house is wider than 24" you will need the 36" length to span the area that isn't broken up by windows and doors. It looks amateurish to piece the 24" lengths. This results in about ten clapboards having the seam in the same place, which would not be the case in real life.

To determine how many pieces of siding you will need for your house, measure the width and height of the sides to be covered. On a side with a gable, measure to the highest point. Multiply the height times the width to get the area.

Measure the height and width of one piece of siding. Multiply the two dimensions and divide the house area by this figure. The answer is the number of pieces of siding you will need. Add an extra piece or two to allow for waste.

Once in a while you may encounter a house with side walls of a size that will cause a lot of waste. When this occurs it is better to measure the side with the siding and see if the off-cuts may be used in spaces between doors and windows on the front. Try fitting the walls with both 24" and 36" pieces.

The clapboard milling in the thin siding boards makes them tend to curl. To counteract this you will need to use Quick Grab glue to attach the siding to the shell. Another way of overcoming this trait is to seal both sides of the siding with shellac before attaching it to the house with solvent-base glue. Clamp, tape, or weight the siding securely while it dries to keep it flat. Paint the siding after it's glued to the house.

If your dollhouse kit manufacturer offers pre-cut siding, as was the case with the Twelve Oaks model, use it. It doesn't cost much more and saves you a lot of time.

HOW TO APPLY CLAPBOARD SIDING

There are two ways to apply wood siding. The realistic way is to install the siding between moldings like the corner trim and window or door surrounds. An easier way is to install the siding first and apply the moldings over it. Your directions will usually recommend the most satisfactory installation for your kit.

If you must make the decision yourself, use your windows as a guide. If the thickness of the window unit allows space for the siding to be slid under the molding, use the easy method. On a die-cut house you can place the siding under the moldings but you will have to fill the telltale seams along the inside edge of the window moldings. Some adjustment will have to be made on the corners, too.

The realistic installation will appeal to you if you're intensely interested in architecture. It does require cutting around window moldings, which is a tiresome job on an ornately trimmed house.

TOOLS NEEDED:

- Work space long enough to accommodate the lengths of siding
- A craft knife with a sharp (new) #11 blade
- A metal straightedge at least 4" long.
- A cutting board and a scrap of siding to cut on.

Begin your work on one of the sides—the easiest one to cover. Apply siding from the bottom of the house upward. The notched edge of the siding is the bottom.

Sheet siding has an idiosyncrasy. The milled clapboards all have slightly rounded edges except for the last board at the

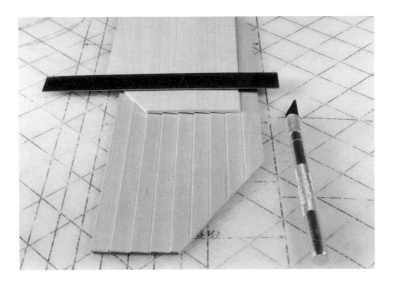

Lay the piece of siding to be cut on top of a scrap of siding so the pieces mesh together. This prevents the edge of the cut from splintering.

notched edge. This one needs to be lightly sanded to make it conform to the rest. If this board isn't rounded, it becomes obvious when the sided house is painted. There will be a line across the wall every place this unsanded board occurs.

Hold the piece of siding up to the house and mark where it should be cut. To prevent the siding from splintering or chipping as you cut it, lay it right side down on a scrap piece of siding lying right side up, the pattern running in the opposite way from the top piece.

The easiest way to work with the knife is to make several strokes until it cuts through, rather than trying to cut it with one stroke. Heavy pressure tends to make you lose guidance control. Cut as many pieces as needed to fill the space from bottom to where the gable slant starts.

Fill the overlap notch of the first piece with a supporting piece of stripwood, especially if the siding starts at the bottom edge of the house. The pre-cut siding comes with this overlap notch trimmed away. When the siding starts above the base, you may use a drip trim instead. Drip trim is a piece of stripwood laid along the top of the foundation. The piece of siding rests on top of it.

Apply glue to the back of the siding. Run a bead of glue ½" from the edge all the way around the perimeter. Fill in the middle so that when the glue is smashed against the house it will flatten out and form a thin film. A thin coat grabs quickly. Clean up any oozes of glue while it is still damp. Use

Use an abundance of masking tape to clamp the siding to the house. When the glue is dry, remove the tape immediately, so it doesn't leave gummy marks on the wood.

masking tape or clamps to hold the siding until it's set.

Carefully place the first piece of siding. Use a square to check that the piece is running a true horizontal. Apply the next and succeeding pieces the same way, always fitting the overlap notch on the top edge of the preceding piece.

When you reach the gable, cut the siding pieces on an angle. Place the piece of siding so that its notched edge fits tightly in place. Mark the back of the siding board with the pattern of the gable at the front and back roof lines. Using a craft knife, cut along these lines.

If the front roof is already on the house, use a piece of paper to make a pattern of the angle. Set the straight edge of the paper along the top edge of the last siding piece and, with your fingernail, score the paper where the edge of the wall and the roof meet. Use this paper pattern as a guide for cutting the front roof line on the siding. After cutting, slip the siding in place on the house. Since the back roof is not on the house, you can easily mark the second edge of the siding, using the wall as a guide.

When you side the front of the house, match the clapboards at the corner. Often a porch on the front interferes with placement of the siding. Cut out the bottom edge to fit around it.

As you work up the front of a house, you will find you can use shorter off-cuts to fill spaces between windows and doors. Be sure to keep a true horizontal line going when you do this. When you reach the space between the first and second floor windows, use a long piece of siding that lines up on all the off-cuts.

In areas where siding pieces partially cover openings, hold or tape it in place and mark the spaces to be cut away from the wrong side. A perfect fit is not necessary when the edges of the siding will be covered by corner trim and component moldings. At the top edge of the wall, make sure the siding conforms to the bevel needed for the roof installation. End the siding a little short of the bevel or trim it off following the contours of the wall edge.

After all the siding is applied and the glue is thoroughly dry, give it a final finish with the recommended paint or stain.

BRICK AND STONE

The easiest-to-apply material for brick walls on a dollhouse is a grid and plaster product called Magic Brik, or plastic panels of embossed brick. For chimneys and foundations, use wooden brick strips, Magic Brik, or the plastic panels. These may be also used for hearth or entry steps.

For a stone finish for walls, use Magic Ston or apply sheets of stone-embossed plastic to be painted. Use these products or individual stones and mortar to cover chimneys, foundations, hearths, or entryway steps.

Use the instructions for applying plastic sheet flooring (Chapter 11) to install the embossed plastic sheet brick or stone. The

The two front walls on the Newport were laid next to each other, and the grid covered both in one continuous strip.

only addition to those directions is to interlock the sheets when adding panels. With a stone finish, trim around individual stones and fit the panels together. For brick panels to interlock, the vertical seams have to be custom trimmed.

To make the panels look more realistic, add more color with acrylic paint. Follow the suggestions given for the Magic Systems and the wooden brick strips.

APPLYING MAGIC SYSTEMS GRID PLASTER PRODUCTS

Use the same method for the all the patterns in the Magic Systems. Each kit contains an adhesive paper grid with a peel-off backing and a plaster-like powdered substance to cover the area marked on the box.

The kits recommend mixing the powder with water to spread over the grid. When dry, the product must be coated with clear acrylic to make it permanent. After it has been mixed with water and allowed to dry, the powder may be reactivated by adding water to it. This is helpful when you are covering a lot of area, because you can reuse waste pulled off the house when you remove the grid. However, using the product this way doesn't give a very permanent finish, as it's easily knocked off the dollhouse.

There is a better way:

Mix white water-base glue and water in the powder instead of just water. Use Tacky glue, mixed 1 part water to 2 parts glue, or Elmer's, mixed 1 part water to 3 parts glue.

Add it, a little at a time, into enough powder to do the job at hand. Make it the consistency of a spreadable cake icing.

Spread the mixture on the house to a depth of $\frac{1}{16}$".

Let it set up and remove the grid. Pull it off when the plaster material will hold its shape and becomes a little dull in appearance. When the brick dries, it cannot be reactivated. It doesn't seem to need a clear acrylic finish.

Another way to use this product is to mix acrylic paint with it. Do this when you want to change the basic color. The paint acts as an adhesive. Use the glue-water mixture if you need more moisture. The product mixed with acrylic paint cannot be reactivated when it's dry, either.

As a novice you will probably be wondering when to remove the grid on this product. Although the instructions give five minutes as a guideline, it's better to check how well the plaster has set and then make the decision. In an inconspicuous corner, pull away the paper grid. If the plaster product stays put and has a stand-up edge, it is time to remove the grid. If the plaster product doesn't stand up, it will probably run and the brick or stone will puddle together. It helps to work with the surface in a horizontal position when possible.

The stone grid runs top to bottom on this chimney. The masking tape mask is also a handle for pulling the grid off after the plaster mix is applied.

Paint the acrylic paint "mortar" on the house and allow it to dry for several days. Then, when you apply and remove the paper grid, the paint won't come off too.

There's also a trick to peeling the grid from the backing paper. Once you get the grid started, hold the backing part flat and pull the grid at a very sharp angle. The acute bend in the grid seems to make the bricks stay on the backing and allows only the mortar grid to come free.

If some of the bricks stay in the grid, remove them before sticking the backing down. The bricks will readily stick to your fingers if you work from the sticky side.

To help this product look realistic, add some extra color to it after it's dry. Experiment with a sample board before using it on your house. Here are some of the ways it was used on the examples in this book:

The brick on the Heritage model was dry-brushed with the lightest shade of red used on the exterior house trim. Dry-brushing means to put a little amount of paint in your brush bristle tips and lightly drag it across the brick surface. Do it randomly. Realism is never symmetric.

When working on the front of the Newport, I finished the front walls before they were attached to the house. I laid them side by side on the work table and laid the mortar grid across both walls at the same time. Because the windows and moldings had to be inset in the brick, I made pencil tracings around all the trims. When spreading the plaster product on the walls, I stopped at all the markings. After the brick was dry I scraped any excess off carefully, so the windows, door, and trims fit flush to the walls.

The stone on the English cottage chimney was originally a grayed white. I painted several complementary browns, beiges, and grays on individual stones. Then I brushed a dirty-water wash over all once the stone paint was dry. (For a wash I used the brush-cleaning water.) If the first coat isn't dark enough, add more coats, but don't make them even.

WOOD BRICK STRIPS

As the name implies, this brick is made of a wood strip; each strip is the height of one brick plus mortar. The length of the strip is 24"; it is scored to look like a line of bricks. The ones used in the book are made by Real Good Toys.

Color the brick strips before cutting them and gluing them to the house. Figure out how many strips you will need for your project. Lay them out on a piece of freezer wrap, so that you can work on them all at once. Don't seal the wood—whatever roughness appears simulates brick texture.

First, put down an irregular coat over the strips with a thinned-down coat of the base color. In the example, this was a coat of storm gray and then a coat of burnt sienna. It was very splotchy, some places being gray and some sienna. Let it dry thoroughly.

Use a sponge to add more color. Dampen the sponge slightly and use a palette knife to smear paint on it as if you were buttering a piece of bread. Just coat the sponge so that you can still see it through holes in the paint. Dab the paint over the wood strips in a spotty fashion. This was done with adobe color, mustard gold, and cream. These colors picked up the color of the siding and porch on this house. Let them dry thoroughly before gluing them to the house.

There is a pattern that must be maintained when laying this brick. Each row should be staggered by half a brick. At the outside corners, each row must have a whole brick on one surface and a half brick adjacent to it around the corner on the second side. The brick strip corners are mitered toward the inside.

To start laying the brick strips, begin at an outside corner. Have the mortar edge up and miter the strip at the beginning of a full brick. Glue it in place with Quick Grab. Starting at the same corner and working in the opposite direction, begin the row with a miter in the middle of the brick. Work row by row until the area is covered. Splice strips at the mortar lines. Let dry thoroughly.

The final touch is to apply mortar. The best product to use for this is Red Devil's "One-Time Spackling"—spackle normally used to fill holes in the wall before painting.

Work one area at a time. Apply spackle with a palette knife, putty knife, or scrap of thin wood. Spread it thoroughly over one area, making sure it gets in all the mortar crevices. Remove most of the excess with

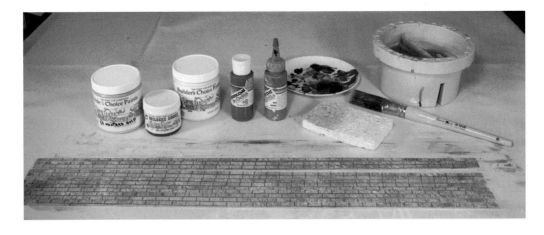

These tools and paints are used to color the brick strips.

At the corner the brick pattern must be a whole brick in one direction and a half brick in the other.

your spreading tool, then burnish the area with a rag. Try to wipe off the bricks, but leave mortar in the grooved crevices. The bricks don't come totally clean, giving them a realistic look.

STUCCO

When you think of applying stucco to a house, you usually think of some type of pasty, plastery compound to be smeared on the surface and swirled around. There are such products out there—artist's modeling paste, joint compound, water putty, Magic Stucco, to name a few. They all take a lot of time to apply. Most of them introduce excess moisture to the surface of the dollhouse, which can cause warping. Many of the products will crack if the house wood expands and contracts. The superior dollhouse stucco is made with acrylic latex paint and a fine-textured grit additive.

To make paint stucco like that used on the English cottage, use off-white paint and Bondex Fine Texture grit. Greenleaf's

Stucco powder may be used in place of the Bondex. Mix the stucco in a separate container from the paint can. Pour as much paint as you think you will need into the container. Add the grit a spoonful at a time until you have a thick mixture that can still be spread with a brush. Paint it on the house over a white-pigmented shellac base. Paint a second coat if you want the texture heavier. A coat of plain paint seems to be the better choice. When the paint is dry, add the half-timber trim. If the texture is a little too thick under some of the trim, scrape it off in that area with a blunt knife. The paint stucco covers wood blemishes and cracks nicely and fills in tab-and-slot joints. It can also be used to duplicate adobe walls.

The preformed half-timber trim on the cottage came with the kit. I stained it while it was still in die-cut sheets, punched it out, and touched up the edges with stain. When it was dry I gave it a couple of coats of semigloss varnish. It's shinier than a real-life finish, but easier to keep clean.

If you want to add your own half timber trim to a house, use $1/16"$ x $3/8"$ bass stripwood. Stain it walnut and apply a clear final finish. Then cut the pieces to fit and glue them over the paint stucco finish. Usually the timber trim outlines windows and doors. A beam is at the floor line and at the bottom and top of the wall. Upright trim comes from under each window. This line is frequently extended upwards from each window, too. That is just a beginning pattern for timber trim. If you want a more detailed half-timber design, consult an architectural book from the library.

When you've given the final finish to the house's exterior walls, you are ready to attach the front roof. The important thing is to have the wall area that will touch the roof sections done, so you don't have to try to paint under angled eaves. On the gable sides there is usually a finishing board that will hide the seam between wall and roof. Attach it after the roof is completely installed.

All the face edges of the Tudor grid may be painted at the same time with one swipe of a wide paintbrush.

7 PREPARING AND INSTALLING THE FRONT ROOF

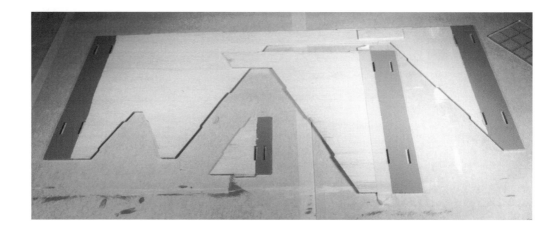

Save time and cleanup by using masking tape to delineate between eaves and ceiling.

Before preparing the roof of the shell, you may want to skip to the chapter on shingling and read through it. Details mentioned there will influence what you do here.

PRIME THE ROOF AND PAINT THE EAVES

Examine how your house roof will go together. You can use the smoother side for the exterior if the pieces are symmetric, no edges are beveled, and you are using a painted finish. If you are planning to cover the roof with another material, put the smoother side to the inside. If the roof pieces are irregularly shaped or if they have beveled edges, you must put them together according to the directions in the kit.

When you hold the roof on the shell you will notice that it overhangs the walls and forms eaves. The underside of the eaves must be stained or painted. On many real houses the eaves are painted a color to coordinate with the house or are brown from creosote. On dollhouses, however, they are usually painted white.

Temporarily fit the roof to the house and mark where the walls meet the roof. Using pencil and working from the inside of the house, draw the lines on the interior roof. Prime the interior surface with white-pigmented shellac. If the eaves will be painted, use the white-pigmented shellac. If there is to be no fascia board, finish the edges of the roof the same as the eaves. Otherwise, leave it bare wood.

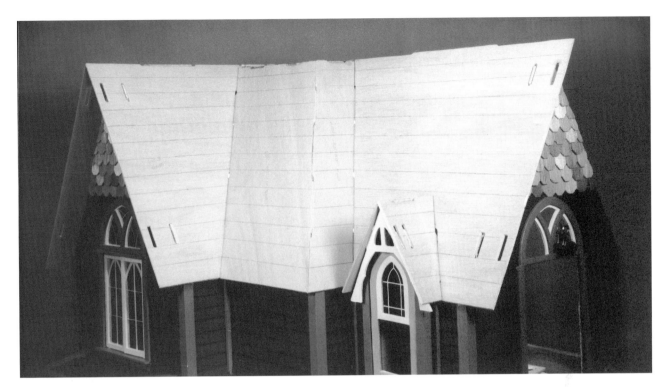

The grid lines, which were drawn before the roof pieces were installed, match up nicely.

It helps to use masking tape along the pencil line to delineate eaves from the inside ceiling. If the whole surface will have a coat of white-pigmented shellac, apply the tape to the inside edge of the line and give a final finish to the eave side. With stained eaves, apply the tape to the eave edge of the line and shellac the inside area. Then move the tape to the shellacked side of the line and stain and varnish the edges. If the tape removes a little of the shellac, that's no problem. Wallpaper will cover it.

Prime the exterior of the roof with clear shellac. Maintain the natural wood finish, so it doesn't show through shingles.

GRID THE SHINGLE AREA

While the roof is still unattached to the house, draw guide lines on it for installing individual or strip shingles. Sheet material doesn't need this preparation.

Refer to the packaging on your shingles for the spacing dimensions to be marked on the roof. If the packaging recommends no specific measurements, take the measurements from your shingle material. Kits that include roof shingles will have dimensions in the instructions.

The rule of thumb is that the spacing between rows is equal to half the length of the shingle. This way the vertical slits between individual shingles show roofing, not the surface of the shell.

Asphalt roll shingles are 1" wide, which means that rows are spaced ½" apart. The average wood shingle is 1¼" long, making the spacing half of 1¼", or ⅝". It works and looks good visually.

Thicker wood shingles can be spaced in rows even farther apart. Because of their thickness, it improves their appearance to have a space of ¾" to ⅞" between rows. If you use the wider spacing, leave no vertical gap between individual shingles.

There's plenty of room for artistic license with the space between rows. Lay out several rows on your work table and choose what you think looks good with your house. Sometimes wider spacing is fine because the dollhouse trim is chunky. Closer spacing looks better with fine line trim. Read ahead in your directions and find out if there is a fascia board (trim) along the bottom edge of the roof. This will affect your spacing.

If your house has a slanted back roof and you want to add a clear acrylic cover to the open space, read the directions for adding it to your house in Chapter 13. The clear acrylic latch will affect the lower roof edge.

The other factor that must be taken into consideration is how the row at the ridge of the roof will finish. Some kits include a

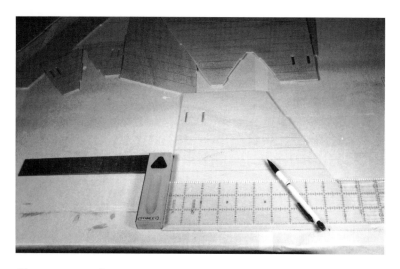

The try square, along the edge of the roof, acts as a base for the ruler to rest against when you draw the spacing line for the shingles.

shingles. The shingles will meet along the ridge and the molding glues over them. The top row of shingle should show approximately the same amount as the spacing, within ⅛" one way or the other.

Another way to finish the roof ridge is the one shown on the Heritage sample house. Place a piece of dowel along the spine of the roof and lay stripwood on either side of it, thus covering the top edges of the shingles.

The last ridge finish imitates a real-life one. Individual shingles are folded in half and overlapped over the seam where the two roof's shingles come together. The top row of shingles should show about the same amount as the spacing for the other rows.

Lay out the main roof pieces on your work table with the bottom edge of each section closest to you. You should have a front and back. Don't worry about gables just yet.

Work the front roof first. At the bottom edge, mark the full length of a shingle. Have the shingle just barely overhanging the edge, by less than ⅟₁₆". A larger overhang will break easily.

Mark the row spacing for your shingles on a thin strip of paper. Hold it against the roof and see if this spacing positions the top row within a reasonable distance from the roof ridge. Usually it does.

ridge trim. One that is often used is an ornate trim that is glued into the middle of the ridge seam. The house roofs are not overlapped and there is a small gully to seat the trim in. The last row of shingle, which rests against it, should be about the width of the spacing used on the roof.

Sometimes the roof ridge is a simple corner molding that fits over the top row of

The right front roof on the Glencroft has a slight curve to it. This required extra care when gluing the roof in place.

Using the paper measuring strip as a guide, make pencil marks along the one side of the roof. Line up the T-square with the marks and draw the grid lines all the way across the roof.

Do the same with the back roof. If it sits under the front roof, make allowance for the width of the front piece.

Hold the gable pieces to their positions against the main roof and mark a starting point for their grids. The back roof on the Glencroft had an unusual slant. It wasn't parallel to any reference point. I drew the grid slanted between the two main back pieces so rain would run off the roof.

This step may seem a little complicated for the first-time builder, but it is a time saver. If you discover later on that you didn't get it quite right, don't panic. With the initial parallel lines laid out, it is easy to make the adjustments when the time comes to apply the shingles.

Use carpenter's glue to fasten the front roof to the house according to the directions in the kit. The tongue-and-groove and tab-and-slot houses have the roofs glued on. Glue and nail the roof to the pre-cut plywood house. Use masking tape and clamps as needed to hold them in place until the glue is dry.

ROOF ON THE FRONT-OPENING HOUSE

If you are working on a house with a front wall and roof that open, you will finish it differently. Most of the time the roof is hinged to the house and lifts up to rest on top. Take care to assemble this part so when the roof is closed it fits in place without unseemly gaps.

Prime the pieces of the roof in the usual way. If the house has a mansard roof, finish the flat ceiling area with white acrylic paint as usual. In a house with a peaked roof, you'll probably wallpaper the ceiling as part of the walls. Finish the eaves as you would on a back-opening house.

Decorate the inside of the front roof the same as the front wall of the house. In the example shown, the front roof was finished with white acrylic paint.

One very important step must be completed as you construct this roof. Always finish the hinged edges completely before actually adding the hinges. Since these edges are usually crosscuts, they are frequently rough. You'll have to seal them with shellac or glue, sand, and then apply a final finish.

Most of the time, the front roof will have dormers. It is vastly simpler to build the dormers, finish them completely, and attach them to the front roof before it is attached to the house.

The finished mansard roof on the Newport.

Study the details in finishing the top floor of this house. The molding is around the dormer opening, since there was no space for it around the window. The flooring is recessed and has crosspieces to delineate the rooms.

There is no hard and fast rule about how to finish the dormers. Their exterior walls may be just about anything. They may match the wall treatment of the body of the house or be shingled like the roof. Sometimes the dormer walls are finished with a metal sheathing. This is used often on a brick house; it is then painted to match the roof or roof trim. The example in this book has painted walls, matching the other trim on the roof.

The roof of dormers may be shingled like the rest of the roof. It may also be metal sheathed and painted to match the roof. In the case of a dollhouse, you don't have to put actual metal on the roof—just paint the wood.

How the inside of the dormer is finished is determined by the decor of the house and how much of the dormer wall can be seen when looking in the windows. With shallow dormers, just paint the walls the same color as the woodwork. If the window is curtained, the walls won't even be visible, so it's sensible to paint the walls. On deep dormers where the walls are visible, finish them with the same wallpaper as is in the

room. You can use a wallpaper finish in the dormer, even if the interior front roof is simply painted.

Glue windows in place and finish the inside moldings. Attach the front roof to the house after the interior of the house is totally finished. You may find it necessary to tape the front roof in place while adding the rest of the roof to the house. This helps with sizing and provides space for the roof. Don't put the hinges on until all the work is done.

When you lay flooring in the top floor of a house with a mansard roof, you will probably need to trim it back the width of the front roof wall; the flooring interferes with the fit of the roof wall. In the picture, you can see that the width of the wall and the top of the house frieze were painted to match the interior woodwork.

On a mansard roof, the top flat surface is usually painted black. Do this painting and put the shingles on the sides and front roof before adding any edge trim.

Lay out the shingle grid on the roof before installing the dormers. Add the grid while the roof pieces are still flat on the work table.

The example had an unusual construction pattern in that the whole top section was constructed and then added to the house. Because of this, the main body of the house was decorated inside and out before the top section was added to the house.

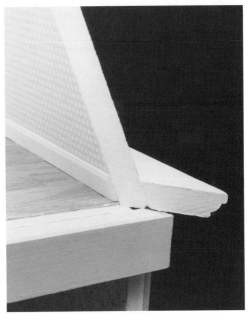

Above: The top section is glued together and squared up. Below: Give the edges a final finish before attaching the hinges to the roof. Trim the flooring out of the area where the roof meets the house.

8 WIRING

Full details on how to install lighting systems, both tape and round wire, can be found in my book, *Dollhouse Lighting*. There you will find complete instructions for installing the systems and fixtures. This chapter discusses different wiring designs in dollhouses of varying construction. It will also update a few of the more important installation techniques.

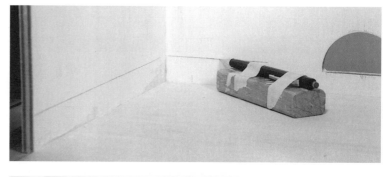

Top: Use a marking tool to draw the wiring guidelines. Bottom: Make the spacing block on the outside of the house about 2" long. If a junction splice is accidentally loosened, there is more space to reattach the splice.

Some general guidelines will help you to create a reliable electrical system. First of all, try to make as few splices as possible. When working with tape wire, use folded corners rather than cutting the tape. A tape wire that runs through the whole house without a break is the ideal. Since the ideal isn't usually possible, plan for the splices to fall where they will be accessible for repair if necessary.

Try to keep the wiring hardware inside the house without running over open edges. If wiring is on exposed edges that can be knocked or picked at (by children and pets), there is a greater chance that it will be damaged.

Tape wire is easy to install. Round wire requires more time and effort. It also seems to be harder to find the correct gauge wire to use. In the miniatures market, very fine wire that will support electricity safely for two or three bulbs is readily available. The next wire commonly stocked is usually the gauge for a lead-in wire. This is too big for feeder lines within the house. It's hard to hide. If you can find the proper gauge wire, become comfortable using it. Just don't hook up too many lights to the fine wire. If it gets hot, the insulation can melt, and a short can occur.

Refer to your notes for your planned fixture placement. Use brightly colored self-stick labels to mark their location in the dollhouse. A pattern usually appears, and you can mark the walls with pencil linking the outlet spots.

To make guidelines for the baseboards (skirting) along the walls, use a marking tool made by taping a pencil to a scrap block of wood. The pencil line should be 1" above the floor. When you have the wiring hardware in, make templates of the rooms showing where the tape runs and where the splices are.

Use tracing paper and mark each template with the room direction, i.e., right room, 1st floor, right wall. Save these templates with the house notebook and papers. Later, after you install the wallpaper, you can lay the template against the wall to find the tape or splices.

Once you have traced the hardware, give the tape wiring a coat of white-pigmented shellac. Then the wiring won't show through the wallpaper.

When you are installing the junction splice on the side of the house, you will probably find it necessary to add a small scrap of wood under the splice. On the Glencroft and the Heritage it helped make the wall thick enough to support the screw that holds the splice in place.

On the Twelve Oaks, I used a piece of siding to make a flat surface for the splice. I reversed the scrap of siding so that the siding side interlocked with the house siding, and I installed the splice on the smooth side facing out.

Install most lights after you wallpaper the room and install trim like moldings, doors, and windows. The exceptions are wall lights and sconces, including exterior coach lights, and ceiling fixtures. The easiest way to install these is to carry the wires through a hole in the wall and connect them to the wiring system on the back side. Sometimes you must connect the wires on the face side. Detailed directions for doing this are in *Dollhouse Lighting*.

Since the various styles of construction in the kits offers some unique opportunities for illustrating possible wiring schemes, we will look at them individually.

TWELVE OAKS

With its center hall configuration and tightly fitting floors, this house is wired by running the tape wire in from one side, skirting the rooms, and taking the primary run up the staircase wall and through the top floor. I started on the side farthest from the staircase opening so that the tape would run around the front door for the outside lights. This primary tape runs up the staircase wall to the top floor. There it continues around the hall wall and through the room to the side wall, where it ends at the midway point.

The second floor tape starts midway on the far wall in one extension room, skirts the wall, and goes through the hall. It ends in the opposite side extension room midway on the farther side wall. This tape crosses the primary tape on the staircase wall, and a splice is made here.

On the first floor, the tape is spliced to the primary tape in the hallway and then continues through the rooms that haven't been wired.

Since I wanted to install ceiling fixtures through the ceiling, tape wire is installed on the floor above the light and connected to the baseboard tape in that room. All this is hidden by the carpeting and wallpaper.

GLENCROFT

Think "circle" when planning this house's wiring scheme. With its tab-and-slot construction, there are slight crevices between floors and walls just wide enough to slip the tape wire through.

Start on the side where the tape enters the house and thread it through all the crevices, from the back side of the lower right room's right wall to the upper fireplace opening where it enters the upper right room. From this point, take it through the doorway into the upper left room. Thread it through the crack between the left side wall and the floor and enter the lower left room.

Starting in the lower left room on its right wall at the level of the sconce, stick the tape permanently to the wall. Take it

around the door opening and across the center wall. Then go across the left side wall, almost to the open edge. Here make a folded corner and go through the ceiling crack and into the upper left room. On the left wall make a double folded corner and bring the tape onto the floor. There it turns again and runs to the center wall. Run it at sconce level on the right wall through the doorway and up the left wall of the right room to the level where it will go over the mirror. On that wall drop it down to baseboard level and skirt the room to the fire-

place opening, exit the interior of the house and run it along the back side of the right wall past the flickering fireplace unit and onto the outside stair support at the junction splice.

On die-cut houses, use only brads or solder to splice and install fixtures. Always make sure your connectors have shanks short enough that they won't pierce through the wall and into tape on the back side of the installation. It's easy to make contact with the wrong conductor and cause a short.

INSTALL A FLICKERING FIRE UNIT

This dollhouse has a fireplace cavity, which is perfect for hiding a flickering fire electronic unit. It's an interesting novelty, and can provide enough power for three fireplaces. It may be used to power flickering light strands for Christmas or billboards.

The unit does have an idiosyncrasy. If you attach it to a whole house wiring system, all the lights in the house will flicker slightly, although not as strongly as the fires that are hooked up to the unit. Flickering lights work in this cottage because it is meant to be lit with gaslight. In a house where you want only the fires to flicker, run the flickering unit off a separate wiring scheme and transformer.

To mount this unit in the example I had to make a little bottomless box from scrap ⅜" wood to hold the unit on the wall. I attached it in the space inside the chimney. When all the chimney walls were in place I cut a keyhole opening in the chimney wall large enough to work through and then mounted two stops made from thin scrap plywood inside along the side edges of the opening. Then I replaced the piece that had been cut out of the chimney, but I didn't glue it. The stone work was completed over it. Now if the unit needs service, I can reach it by slicing the stonework with a knife.

HERITAGE

This house needed to be well illuminated so that all the little accessory pieces can be easily seen. It is lit with indirect lighting. The open edge of the house is trimmed with a deep edge molding which helps support and camouflage the baffles. They keep the lights from glaring in the viewer's eyes.

The wiring scheme for this house is simple. The primary run comes in through a slit in the left wall. It goes up the left wall all the way to the attic where it angles at the gable and runs across the top of the front roof wall. On the ceiling sides of the second and third floor pieces, one strip of wiring runs the full width and is connected at the left wall.

The wiring hardware was laid in the ceiling before the floors were installed in the

This is how the "fire" wires are distributed to the fireplaces in the Glencroft.

The keyhole opening in the chimney before it was sealed under the Magic Ston.

house. The baffles are ¾" strips of basswood, sealed and painted white. I glued aluminum foil to the baffles where the fluorettes are installed to make them opaque and reflect the light into the house room. The fluorettes are tube-shaped lights rated as "super bright." Each is equivalent to three or four bulbs on the transformer.

On this house, there is a 24-bulb strand of Christmas tree lights outlining the porch

trim. The wires from this were brought in the second floor French window and run along the second floor seam to the primary run of tape wire.

NEWPORT

This style of house is usually made of ⅜" plywood or MDF board. It's the usual type of dollhouse in England and reflects the development in Europe from the baby house or cabinet house of the seventeenth and eighteenth centuries. These baby houses were cupboards for adult miniature

Above: To maintain a continuous run of wire to the third floor, the excess is stored on the end post while the lower floors

Right: The wiring tape and wires have been enhanced with black marker to show where the wires came out the back wall and were connected.

collections and were a sign of your wealth.

Present-day front-opening dollhouses are among the easiest to wire. Run all the wires from the fixtures through the back wall first. Then lay the tape wire in a continuous piece coming within reach of all the fixture wires. Start the tape on the back wall at the base of the house close to one of the sides. Run it horizontally for a short distance so the junction splice can be connected conveniently. Make a folded turn and run the tape up the wall, centering it between the fixture wires on that side of the back. Turn at the top floor and come down the other side of the back wall, centering the tape between the fixture wires on that half of the back. When it's done, the tape forms a big inverted U on the back of the house. Connect the fixtures, and the house is lit.

After the fixtures are connected to the system, tape all the wires down with Scotch Magic Tape. Doing so prevents snagged wires and disconnected lights. Finally, you can cover the wiring system with a piece of mat board or plywood cut to fit the back of the house.

The grooves show the path of the two lead wires as they split to go through the middle and bottom hinges on the door.

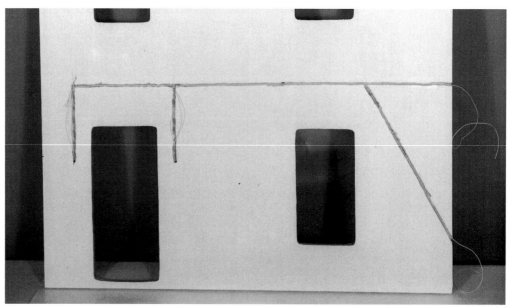

The Newport has lights on the front wall. I took the wiring through the hinges to provide electricity for the coach lights either side of the door. Because the wall will be painted, I used round wiring hidden in a groove that is filled with spackling paste.

HINTS FOR CONNECTING FIXTURES

Clare-Bell Brass, one of the oldest lighting manufacturers, has changed the wiring in some of their fixtures. The double candle sconce pictured illustrates the change. To get the wires through the tiny tubing, it is necessary to remove the insulation on one of the wires. In a two-bulb fixture like this one, the two insulated wires are twisted together and the two bare wires are likewise joined, then connected to the tape wire as shown.

Installing coach lights on clapboard siding is a nuisance because of the texture of the siding. It's sometimes difficult to make enough contact between the light and the siding to support the weight of the fixture. A scrap piece of siding turned upside down and wrong side out and placed between the light and the siding will make a firm surface for the connection. The plates behind the coach lights on the Twelve Oaks were made from siding. I cut out two rectangles of siding and snipped the corner off with a round-hole paper punch. I glued them in place and installed the coach lights over them. The same thing could be done with the siding cut to fit the back plate on the light, and the filler piece would be almost invisible.

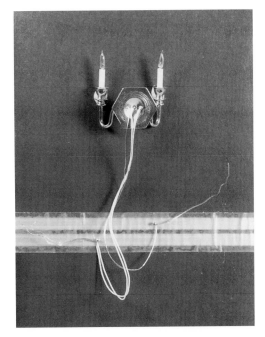

Left, above: This two-light fixture appears to have three leads instead of four. The two bare wires are twisted together and appear as one. This is connected to one tape wire lead, and the two insulated wires are connected to the other. Below: This coachlight is mounted on a siding backplate.

9 WOOD FLOORING

This and the following four chapters deal with decorating the interior of your dollhouse. It's a good idea to take a few minutes now to read through these chapters and plan how you will attack the project. Lighting fixtures and special wall treatments may mean you will be installing parts out of the normal sequence. It's easy to be so enthusiastic about how one room is progressing that you may want to complete it before going on. When working on a child's dollhouse, you may find that decorating a room at a time is a dandy gift for a special occasion. If you know you have to install a dining room chandelier before you finish the floor above it, you can plan your decorating accordingly.

As a rule of thumb, start your interior decorating on the bottom level of the house. Lay wood floors first, finish the walls, and then lay the remaining floors. Install the doors, windows, and room moldings. Attach the lights.

Most often you can do all of one type of decorating at a time. For example, install all the wood floors and finish them. The exceptions happen when you must plan around installing ceiling or wall lights or decide to use the dollhouse walls as part of your decorating scheme. In the Newport, for instance, I made wainscoting by putting moldings on the wooden wall. The wall had to be primed and painted before I laid the wood floor. I added the panel framing later,

but it should have been installed earlier so it wouldn't have been necessary to mask the floor while I applied the final coat of paint to the wainscoting.

When you are planning around light fixtures, finish a room totally with through-the-ceiling or wall installations before doing adjacent rooms. Always install the moldings before the lights so they aren't hanging in the way. It's so easy to knock a light and cause the bulb to burn out.

INSTALL THE WOOD FLOORING

As wood flooring usually gets its final coats of varnish or paste wax applied in the house, it's a good idea to finish these floors before applying the wall finish. Wallpaper paste will easily wipe off the finished flooring, but getting varnish or wax on wallpaper would ruin it. If you are installing other types of flooring in some of your rooms, wait to do that installation until after you paper or finish the walls. Wallpaper paste would spot those floor finishes.

When you purchase wood flooring for your dollhouse, you will discover that floor planks come in many colors and sizes. This allows for some customized floors if you are so inclined. Late Victorian floors, in particular, were often very fancy, with contrasting borders or inlaid patterns. Present-day homes frequently have patterned floors in the foyer. Research the styles if you want to incorporate this kind of floor.

Historically, the tradition was to lay the finer patterned floors in the state or public rooms, i.e., foyer or front hall, living room, parlor, or dining room. Upper floors, kitchens, and servants' quarters had wider planked, more common wood floors. You may want to reflect that in your dollhouse. It was done in the Twelve Oaks and Newport houses.

Four kinds of wood flooring are used in dollhouses. The simplest was already mentioned in the chapter on assembling the body of the house. That is the floor provided in the kit, stained and varnished. It may be scribed to look like individual boards. The other kinds are paper-backed veneer wood strip flooring, scribed wood flooring, and individual wood strips laid one at a time.

There are a couple of ways to cut the flooring to fit. If the house floor is a basic rectangle, you may measure the dimensions with a carpenter's measuring tape or a strip of paper. Measure the width of the room at both the front and the back, noting if they are the same dimensions. Measure the depth. If you are using a measuring tape, note the dimensions in your dollhouse notebook. If you are working with the paper strips, crease them into the corners. Note in pencil which room and which dimension each is. Do this for all the wood floors you will be laying.

The second way to make a pattern is a "tear and tape" method. This is the routine to use when the floor is complicated with alcoves or bay windows. Notebook paper is a nice weight paper to work with. It has four square corners and is easily creased. You will also need some Scotch tape and a straight-edge to tear the paper against.

Begin making your pattern by laying a sheet of notebook paper in a square corner. If the sheet of paper is bigger than the room, tear it in two, using the straightedge. Replace the pieces in the room so they fit and tape them together. Proceed with the other edges of the room. Tear, fit, and tape pieces until the floor is totally covered. Mark the pattern as to which room it is, where the open edge is, note "This side up," and the fact that it is the floor. Use Scotch tape to attach the pattern to the flooring to cut it.

Use tape on all four sides unless one edge of the pattern is along an edge of the material to be cut. As you cut out the flooring, the tape falls away. This method of pattern making can also be used for carpeting, sheet tile floors, and even wallpaper, when the walls are irregular.

In dollhouses, wood flooring is usually laid with the wood strips running parallel to the open side of the house. This is logical because most of the time the imaginary floor joists would be running front to back. Flooring would run side to side to strengthen the floors.

A piece of flooring should fit the entire width of the floor in a room without piecing. A seam with 6 to 24 boards in a row would be unrealistic.

In some dollhouses there are open doorways with no doors. When this happens, you need some kind of break in the flooring to eliminate the awkward ending of the sheet of flooring. This is easily done by ending the flooring at the edge of the room and laying a board crosswise on the doorway floor. In the adjacent room, proceed with the flooring used there, whether it is wood or carpeting or tile.

Sometimes in an attic it's desirable to leave the whole floor open with no partitions. In this case, since the flooring won't go all the way across, you can make patterned breaks by running a crosswise strip

The "tear and tape" patterns shown were made for some irregular dollhouse walls.

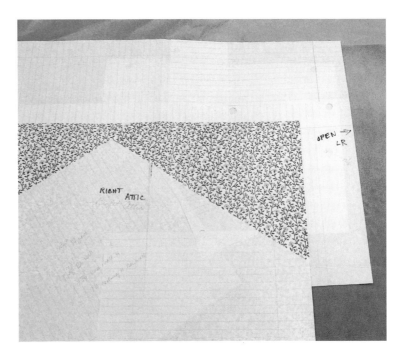

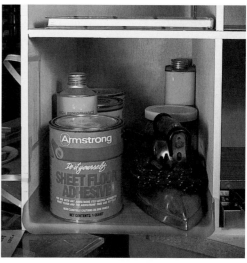

Left, above: A patterned break in a sheet veneer flooring. Right: An old heavy iron makes a good floor weight.

of wood from each corner of the stairway opening out to the open edge of the house.

Another way is to run an area of crosswise flooring. When the flooring ends, usually two thirds of the way across the dollhouse floor, install the remaining floor crosswise to the original. The contrast will act as a delineation for arranging the furnishings in the area.

Always start at the open edge of the dollhouse when laying out your wood floor. Any half boards that may occur in fitting the flooring will be deep in the house and end up under furniture or so far away in the line of vision it will go unnoticed. The exception to this rule is when working with patterned floors. Then it is usually preferable to center the floor so the edges are all the same.

PAPER-BACKED, VENEER STRIPWOOD FLOORING

This popular flooring is realistic and convenient to lay. It is something of a time saver too, since the individual wood strips are already laid on a paper backing. Trim the flooring to fit with a pair of scissors and glue it into place.

Plain paper-backed flooring comes in 11" x 17" sheets. If patterned, it comes in 6" x 8" sheets. Handley House, Houseworks, and Miniature House are popular brands of this type of flooring.

Most of the flooring makers recommend using contact cement to glue the flooring in place. I have found that it's easier to use Quick Grab glue. Run a bead of glue in a

spiral on the paper side of the flooring. When putting it in place in the house, rub the flooring back and forth, further distributing the glue into crevices and eliminating air bubbles. Slide it into its permanent position without lifting it. Roll the floor with a brayer, too. It's important to get a good stick-down, especially around the edges and at the seams. Put waxed paper over it and weight it down with canned goods or books until the glue is dry. To distribute the weight more evenly, put a book or board down under the cans.

I used a light-colored paper-backed flooring in the Newport. Since it was a little too light, I stained it with Minwax's Golden Oak applied with a rag, so the paper back was not saturated. Stain will loosen the paper-back adhesive. Then I sealed the flooring with a thin coat of clear shellac, applied with a brush sparingly. I finished it with a coat of Ceramacoat Water-base Varnish. Since the floors are supposed to appear as if they had been washed and bleached, a dull sheen was all that I wanted. At this point I glued the floors in place and applied the final coat of paste wax with a rag and buffed it to finish.

Since I needed access to the chandelier installation in the floor above the dining room, I had to make a section removable. In the area over the wiring, I cut the flooring, following a board seam from side wall to side wall. The section was about 4" deep. I applied glue only around the perimeter of the backing before putting it in place. If there is ever a problem with the lighting I

*A scribed wood floor-
ing in the Twelve
Oaks house.*

can slip a palette knife blade under the flooring and it will easily come up.

SCRIBED WOOD FLOORING

This flooring comes in 3" x 24", $\frac{1}{16}$" thick basswood pieces. Maple wood is also available, but most shops have it as a special-order item. The scribing on this flooring may be in increments of $\frac{1}{4}$", $\frac{3}{8}$", $\frac{1}{2}$", or random. It's made by two companies, Northeastern and Midwest. It's used in the halls of the sample house, Twelve Oaks.

Scribed wood flooring is similar to the clapboard siding in that it, too, must have the long side edges rounded off slightly. If you don't do this you will have a floor with a wide board every three inches, thereby destroying the realism of the floor.

Another detail you may want to add, especially if you are using this flooring for a room wider than a hall, is some cross scribing randomly done to indicate the end of planks. Use a hard lead, fine point pencil to mark the plank ends. You may also use the pencil to indicate pegs for a rustic look.

Stain the boards the color of your choice. Seal them with one coat of clear shellac. Apply one coat of Ceramacoat Semi-Gloss Varnish. When the boards are dry, cut them to fit the room, starting the flooring at the open edge of the house. Use a straightedge and craft knife to cut the wood. Glue the floor pieces in place with carpenter's glue, then apply the last coat of varnish. To use paste wax at this point may obscure the floor pattern, so I don't recommend it.

Because of the irregularity in the veneer stripes, cut, fit, and glue each row in place before doing the next one.

I made a removable section for access to lighting in the downstairs hall on the second floor. That section of floor covering the splice has glue only on the perimeter of the piece. It too could be easily removed if the lighting needed attention.

INDIVIDUAL WOOD STRIPS

Laying a floor with individual wood strips allows you to design some inlaid floors. It takes more time to do but is rewarding because even simple changes create an impressive look.

Individual veneer wood strips usually come in Dura-craft kits. The directions say there is enough wood to do one entire floor, but the kit used for this book had enough wood to do all three floors.

In Chapter 5, I explained why the porch floorboards in the tongue-and-groove kit needed to change directions. A veneer strip was cut to ¼" width and laid from the house corner to the porch corner to aid in the transition.

The floor could have been interwoven at the corner or finished with a simple miter. With a Victorian style house, fancy wood-work may be any way your whimsy leads you. The bays in this house could have been delineated with a border strip, too. Likewise, a crosswise strip could be used in the arched opening and at all partition openings on the upper floors.

To lay a veneer strip floor, first mark the floors of the house body with parallel lines about every inch or inch and a half. Veneer is not very uniform in width, so you will need the lines to keep the floor from becoming crooked. In the example, I laid the veneer directly on the house floor on the first and second levels. The third floor needed a posterboard liner to fill in some floor gaps. I glued the wood to the liner and the liner to the house after applying the final finish to the surface. I did the second floor the same way.

Use Quick Grab glue to attach the veneer strips to the house floors and the liner. Cut, fit, and glue each row in place before doing the next. Sometimes there will be gaps between the boards. It's okay, but try to keep them to a minimum.

Once the boards are in place, sand them. Wipe off all debris and give the floor a coat

This basswood strip floor has a contrasting darker stripe as a border to the surface.

of paste wood filler. Paste wood filler is a brush-spreadable filler that is wood color. You will usually find it at a full service paint store. It is oil based and fills the rough wood grain and gaps.

After the wood filler has set, but before it is totally dry, rub down the surface with a soft cloth. You will now notice that the wood surface has taken on a definitely smoother feel.

When the surface is thoroughly dry, apply a coat of clear shellac. Rub this down with a piece of brown paper bag. Use your hand rather than your eye to determine how satiny the floor is. The large oak grain in this floor was deceiving. Apply a final coat or two of varnish and rub it down with the paper bag.

Basswood strips may also be used for flooring. They are uniform in size and take stain well. Stain the strips before cutting and fitting them to the floor. Glue them in place with carpenter's glue or Quick Grab. Cover the floor with wax paper and weight it until dry. Apply clear shellac and the final coats of clear varnish.

"MARBLE" TILES

Lay a tile floor, such as the one in the foyer of the Twelve Oaks, before installing wallpaper. Because the hall is so narrow—7 inches wide—it was installed even before the second partition wall. This floor, made by Miniature Manors, is a shiny Formica surface backed with a resin base. Wallpaper paste can be wiped off this surface without marring it.

The tiles are available in several colors. Since they are difficult to cut, it's best to make designs with them from whole tiles. The foyer floor in the Twelve Oaks is seven tiles wide. The second wall was installed against the tile edge, so it wasn't necessary to do any trimming.

Installation is simple. These tiles are laid flush to each other, with no gaps between. I applied carpenter's glue to the back of the tile and smeared it to the edge. Rub the tile

against the floor to get rid of air bubbles and slide it into its spot. Don't lift the tile once you've seated it. Wipe off any excess glue with a damp cloth. Cover the floor with waxed paper and weight it for 24 hours until dry.

Treat individual ceramic tiles the same way. If the tile maker doesn't name a spe-

cific adhesive to use, Quick Grab will do. Lay the tile edge to edge without any spacing. Ceramic tiles are always slightly irregular, and that irregularity provides the in-scale space between them. Use the Red Devil's One-Time Spackling paste as mortar. After the floors are laid and dry, you are ready to wallpaper.

10 FINISHING INTERIOR WALLS

Two creative ways to use wallpaper borders.

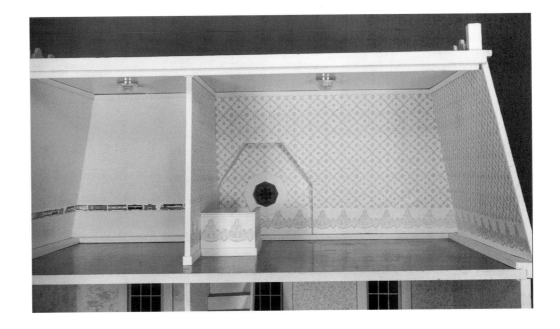

Before you apply any finish to the interior walls, seal them with white-pigmented shellac, covering the tape wiring too, and smooth with a brown paper bag. Remove all debris from inside the house with a dust rag, brush, and vacuum.

If you don't seal the wall, the color of the wood will show through the wallpaper. Moreover, the wallpaper paste will soak into the wood and not allow the paper to stick as it should.

WALLPAPER

Wallpaper is the most common finish for the interior walls of a dollhouse. It helps set an atmosphere and brings your house alive. There are many designs available, some printed especially for dollhouses. Others are "real life" papers that are sold for dollhouse use because of their small patterns.

It's fun to be creative with wallpaper. Instead of using one paper in a room, you may want to try coordinated papers. Use one pattern on one wall and another on the remaining walls, or one on the ceiling and its companion on the walls. Another option is to use a chair rail to divide the walls. Then you can use different papers above and below the rail trim.

Cut apart striped or bordered papers and use the resulting edging as trim around windows and doorways. Sometimes you can use the custom-made border horizontally at the top, middle, or bottom of the wall. Or use it to delineate the shape of dormers and attic walls.

When you purchase wallpaper for your house, try to select all the styles you will want for the entire house at the same time. Lay them out on a table or floor at the store and place them as you would see them in the house. This will help you achieve a balance of color and design.

Usually you will need three sheets of paper per room. You'll need a fourth sheet if you are covering a ceiling in an attic, as in the attic rooms in the Twelve Oaks. If you will cut borders from striped paper, you'll need a fourth sheet for that as well.

With regard to application, the papers fall into two categories. The first is the thin paper printed especially for dollhouses. If you find a gift-wrap paper you want to use, treat it as one of these thinner papers, too.

The second category is pre-pasted wallpaper. This is full-size wallpaper that is sold to be used in the dollhouse. It is heavier, usually with a thin plastic coating. You may also find a wallpaper you like at a decorating center.

"MINIATURE WALLPAPER"

When working with thinner paper you will need clear spray matte acrylic and one of the following: MiniGraphics Wallpaper Mucilage, Grandma Stover's Stickflat Glue (formerly YES glue), Builders' Choice Wallpaper Gel (formerly Milly August Wallpaper Paste) or cellulose wallpaper paste mixed to a thick consistency (1 cup water to 2 tablespoons of dry paste, and even thicker, if necessary). When in England, I used Solvite All Purpose Paper Adhesive as the cellulose wallpaper paste. The Pritt Paper Bond glue is very similar to Grandma Stover's Stickflat Glue.

Never use rubber cement. It turns the wallpaper yellow, and in a short time the paper will curl and come unglued. Rubber cement was never meant to be a permanent adhesive. All of the above holds true for spray adhesive, too.

Before starting your wallpaper project, take the mini paper outside and spray front and back with clear acrylic spray. This seals the printing and makes the paper less absorbent. Since the spray is smelly and flam-

mable, it's best to use it outside. Do all the papers at one time. The spray will dry quickly and you will be able to give it the recommended two or three coats in a few minutes. Put a plastic glove on your holding hand so the spray doesn't build up on your thumbnail.

MiniGraphics Mucilage and Grandma Stover's Glue are similar products. They have a smooth texture and don't seem to penetrate the paper very much. This keeps the mini paper from stretching, as it tends to do. Using a 1½" foam or synthetic bristle brush, spread the glue on the back of the paper, being sure to cover the whole surface. Apply the paper to the wall. Smooth out the air bubbles and trim the paper out of all openings.

The properties of Builder's Choice Wallpaper Gel fall between the "stickflat" types and the cellulose wallpaper paste. At full strength it works just like the stickflats on mini paper. Apply it in the same way.

When you work with cellulose wallpaper paste, you will use a different method. Paint the walls to be covered with a coating of wallpaper paste. With a foam or bristle brush, spread the paste over the surface of the back of the paper. Let it sit for a couple of minutes to see how absorbent the paper is going to be. If it soaks up the paste, give it a second coat. Apply the paper to the wall.

If you are working on a project with foam core or illustration board walls, always use the stickflat type paste on the wallpaper. It minimizes warping in the walls.

PRE-PASTED WALLPAPER

When you buy pre-pasted paper, the salesperson will usually tell you that water will activate the glue on the back surface and it's then ready to be pasted to the wall. Don't believe it! It usually comes loose within a year of installation.

I recommend applying pre-pasted paper with cellulose wallpaper paste mixed 1 cup water to 1 tablespoon of dry paste. This may be mixed thicker if you like. Put a coating of paste on the walls to be covered and a coating on the back of the wallpaper. The wall doesn't have to dry before you apply the paper. If it is dry, the paste will reactivate when the damp paper is put on.

Builder's Choice Gel can be used on pre-pasted paper too. It seems to work better if it's thinned just a bit with water.

APPLYING WALLPAPER

First, prepare a work area for cutting the wallpaper to size, and a separate area for applying wallpaper paste to the paper. At the cutting station you will need an 18" x 24" cutting mat, an Olfa rotary cutter, an Omnigrid 18" x 3" see-through ruler, and a sharp pencil. You may substitute a craft knife with a #11 blade or a single-edge razor blade. However, once you have used a rotary cutter you will be dissatisfied with the knife or razor blade. If your miniature shop does not carry these three tools, you can find them at your nearest quilt fabric store.

The rotary cutter is a fairly new tool on the market. Quilters use it to cut patches for their quilts. The tool is extremely sharp, as it is used to cut several layers of fabric at a time. For safety's sake, keep your fingers back from the edge of the ruler you use with it, and always push the blade guard in place before laying the tool down after making a cut. To use this tool, place it at the edge closest to you and push it away along your straightedge. Conversely, a knife or razor blade cut is started at the edge away from you and pulled toward you.

The clear acrylic rulers sold to use with the cutter are also excellent to use with craft knife or razor blade. They are about 1/4" thick and provide good support for all cutting blades. It's almost impossible to ruin the ruler by shaving off any of its edge, as one can on a wood or thin plastic ruler.

At the second work area, the pasting place, you will need a clean, waterproof 18" x 24" surface like a Formica countertop or a portable piece of 1/4" sheet acrylic, a basin of water, a rag, wallpaper paste, and a 1 1/2" foam or bristle brush.

At the dollhouse you will want a single-edge razor blade and an old charge card or plastic card from a d. Anne Ruff pleater, a damp rag, and a dry rag.

When you wallpaper a room, hide the seams as much as possible. Never have a seam on the center wall, since this is the one surface always in full view. It's best to position the seams on the side wall 1" from the junction of the center and side walls. This seam is usually butted together. Install the

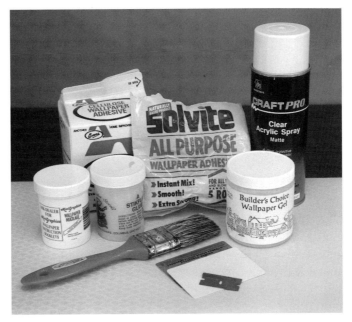

Top: Various pastes and the necessary tools for installing wallpaper. Below: The "pasting station," where wallpaper paste is applied to the paper.

center wall first, and then do the side walls.

Begin with the simplest room—the one with the straightest walls and fewest dormers, bays, or niches. If the walls are straight, you will only need to know the height and width of the left, center, and right walls. Don't measure door and window openings—simply cover them with paper and trim it out.

A carpenter's metal tape measure is best for measuring the height of the room. The width, particularly of the center wall, is usually easiest to measure with a strip of paper, such as the backing paper from the wiring tape. Crease it into one corner, stretch it to the second corner, and crease again. Then lay this strip of paper along the bottom edge of a sheet of wallpaper and move it back and forth to determine the best way to center the pattern of the wallpaper. Write down your dimensions so you don't have to repeat measuring the walls.

A piece of the perforated waste edge from computer paper was used to measure the wall and mark the wallpaper.

Matching the wallpaper pattern horizontally sometimes requires cutting off some paper at the top of the wall.

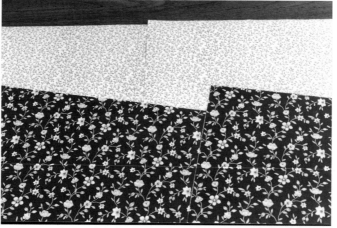

When marking the wallpaper for fit, always start with the center wall. It is usually the wall farthest away from the open edge of the dollhouse and the one most likely to

show the true pattern. If there is a definite vertical pattern, center any opening in that wall with the pattern in the paper, usually having the pattern equally on each side of the opening.

At other times you may need to center the pattern between the two side walls. When you're pleased with the arrangement, make a small light pencil mark on the wallpaper at each end of the center wall. Then add an inch to each side to go around the corner in the dollhouse onto the adjoining walls. An inch is a minimum measurement. You may want to make the measurement greater to increase your chances of matching the pattern in the center to the side pieces at the seam. Mark the back of this piece of paper "C" for center and draw several arrows pointing toward the top of the paper. Do the same with the side pieces, marking the right side "R" and the left "L."

Next, match the pattern of the center piece with the two pieces of wallpaper for the sides. Slide the paper back and forth till you find the exact point where they match. Mark the side papers with pencil at that spot. Measure the amount of usable paper in the side pieces to be sure there is enough to cover the side walls.

Since the height of the room is usually shorter than the paper, decide which edge to cut off. Usually the pattern around the ceiling edge is the one that should be pleasing.

On the mini papers, the top and bottom edges are always printed the same. That's not usually so on pre-pasted paper. Because these sheets have been cut from large rolls, they usually have to be trimmed to a straight edge. The pattern repeat may also need some adjusting.

Measure the height of the room on the paper for the center wall and mark it with a pencil. Does it line up with the paper for the side walls? If it doesn't, work back and forth between the three pieces until you have a horizontal match that still allows for the height of the room. For example, the top edge of the left paper is the ceiling edge in the room. The center piece, in order to match, must have ¼" trimmed off the top. The right piece will need ½" removed at the top. Then measure the height of the room.

After you have marked all the measurements on the paper and re-checked everything, cut the paper using the straightedge and rotary cutter.

Take the papers to the pasting station. Paste and install the pieces one at a time, starting with the center piece. Lay the center piece on the work space, face down. Apply the appropriate wallpaper paste, starting the strokes of paste in the middle and working it to the edges. Apply it evenly and sparingly but still fully covering the surface, including the edges.

Place the wallpaper on the center wall in the room by lining up the top edge at the ceiling seam. Center the paper as you want it, patting the top edge in place first. Working from the center of the paper to the corners, gently pat it into place. Let the excess wallpaper go into the corner and around on the side walls. Pat the edges in place on the side walls. Slide the paper into position when necessary. You'll find the wallpaper paste allows you to do this. When all appears right, smooth the paper in place using the charge card.

Stroke the paper tight to the wall. Start in the middle of the piece and smooth toward the ceiling and floor, then toward the corners and side walls. When you get to the corner, use the edge of the charge card and tap the paper tightly into the corner crevice. Smooth from the corner onto the side wall. At this point some excess paste will probably ooze out. Remove it with the damp rag. Then gently wipe the paper with the dry rag. Double-check the corners to make sure the paper has stayed tight in them. Use a light but firm touch when working with wallpaper. Don't scrub at it with the rags. If you're too zealous you can damage the paper by rubbing the ink off or tearing it.

Cut openings in the wall with a new single-edge razor blade. Begin by making an "X" in the opening with four strokes of the blade. Start in each corner and slash to the center. Wipe the blade clean of paste. To finish trimming, poke a hole in the paper at the center of the side edge. Using the edge of the opening as a guide for the razor blade, slash the paper to the corner while holding the scrap paper taut with the other hand. Do the same from the center to the other corner. That side of the opening is now clean. Wipe the paste off the blade and trim the remaining sides of the opening. Smooth the paper along the edges of the opening to be sure they are tight.

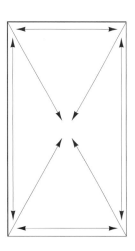

The pattern for trimming an opening in the wall. Do the "X" first, then the perimeter.

The secret to clean cuts is keeping the blade clear of paste and slashing from the center to the corners. Always work with a sharp blade so you won't tear the paper. Do all openings this way.

Install the side pieces of wallpaper. Begin by holding the dry paper in the room and butt the joining edge with the installed paper to see if there is excess width in the side wallpaper—there usually is. Trim the paper so you have only ½" to 1" extra. When you have to trim the open edge after the paper is installed, you want enough to hold while you trim that edge clean with a razor blade.

Apply the wallpaper paste to the side paper as you did before. Slide the paper in place, butting its edge to the center piece of wallpaper and keeping the top edge along the ceiling seam. Gently pat most of the paper in place. Check to make sure the seam is right. Half the time it isn't, and it requires some finagling to make it work. Depending on the pattern, you may have to leave a tiny gap—or part of the seam may have to overlap. Do what must be done. Then, when you are smoothing the seam, make sure the paper is tight to the wall and that all excess paste is wiped off the face of the wallpaper. Trim along the open edge of the room and along any openings for doors or windows.

Do the second side wall the same way and let the wallpaper dry. Don't try the electricity until the wallpaper is dry. Moisture in the paste can cause the lights to short out if you turn them on while the paper is wet.

The walls in the tongue-and-groove houses have corner posts that protrude into the room. These are best just covered with the wallpaper, which usually camouflages their existence. Sometimes, as with the bays in the example in this book, the corner posts can be treated as woodwork. In such a confined area papered posts would not have looked properly finished.

On the second floor in the Heritage, there is a considerable gap between the front roof and the wall. I disguised it with a shelf that filled the space, edging the shelf with a border from the appropriate wallpaper. I cut the border with a pair of scalloping shears.

The center walls in the top floors of the Twelve Oaks are short and extend into the ceiling. That expanse is more than the height of the sheet of wallpaper used. I overcame this problem by making a butt seam where the ceiling and the wall come together. In the room with the border that follows the ceiling seam, I covered the seam joint with the border. In the room with the heart border, the paper matched easily along the ceiling seam and didn't require a cover-up.

These rooms also illustrate how to handle side walls that must be cut separately. In this type of room, measure the center wall, adding an extra ¼" to each side to accommodate covering the corner. Make patterns of the side walls, using the tear-and-tape technique that you used for the wood floor.

When measuring the wallpaper for this type of room, do the center wall first. Cut the side walls exactly the same size as the pattern. Try to match the corners to the short center wall. Where a slanted wall is involved, the pattern cannot be matched. When installing the wallpaper, you'll find the side walls will overlap the small extensions of the center wall covering, which cover the corner seams.

Rooms with dormers are a real challenge. Each one will be a little different, but there are a couple of guidelines that will help when you're planning how to paper such a room.

First, use a wallpaper with an all-over pattern that doesn't need careful matching.

Always plan your wallpapering method to work the deepest wall surfaces first—usually somewhere in the center wall. In the dormer, make a pattern of the deepest surface allowing for a ¼" extension of paper on all edges except along the floor side. The extensions will cover corner seams. Install this piece of paper first.

Make patterns of the side walls of the dormer. Sometimes the side walls are taller

Look in the corners to see how well the wallpaper camouflages the necessary corner posts.

than the sheet of wallpaper. In that case, make a break where the side wall runs into the slanted ceiling. When making the pattern for the side wall, add a ¼" extension to the edge along the outside corner of the wall and at the peak of the dormer. Then when you install the paper, wrap it around the corners and onto the slanted roof surfaces. When you make patterns for the slanted roof surfaces, the edges along the dormer openings will overlap the pieces on the dormer's side wall.

When the basic wallpaper is dry, apply any borders you want to add. Use the baseboards or architectural details to guide you in getting the borders on straight. If you're using a border as a chair rail, cut a template of cardboard that you can use as a guide in placing the border. Sometimes it's better to wait until the wood moldings are installed to apply the paper borders.

FABRIC WALL COVERING

Sometimes you may want to cover the walls with fabric instead of wallpaper. You can do this by using a posterboard or mat board liner, attaching the fabric to the liner and gluing it in place.

When preparing the fabric for the walls, cut and fit the center wall first, then the side walls. Measure the height and width of the wall on the cardboard. Then subtract at least ¹⁄₁₆" from each measurement. You may have to subtract a larger amount if the fabric you are going to use is bulky. Trace and cut out the openings for doors and windows. If there are moldings to go around openings, they will show a gap where the

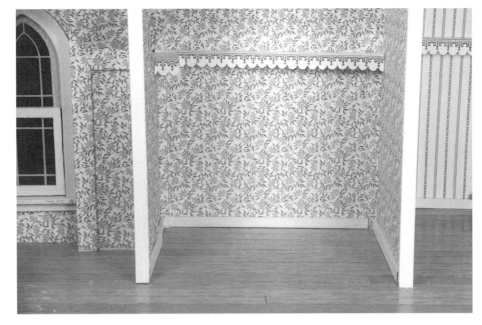

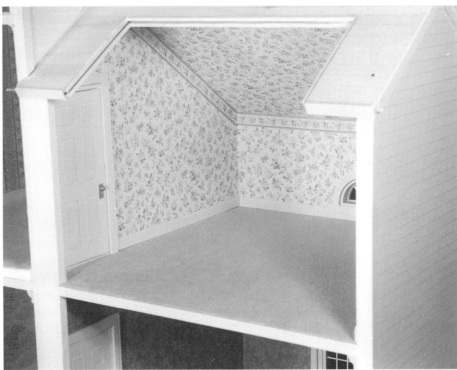

fabric and liner are. This gap may be filled with spackling paste.

Cut the cardboard liner to fit the wall. When it is right, use it to cut the fabric. (First press the fabric to eliminate any wrinkles.)

Work on the cutting board that goes with a rotary cutter. Lay the liner right side up on the fabric, which is also right side up. Move the liner back and forth until the design on the fabric is centered. Using a rotary cutter and the see-through ruler, cut

Top: The shelf with the wallpaper edging covers a gap between wall and ceiling. Bottom: The ceiling border was cut from a coordinating striped wallpaper.

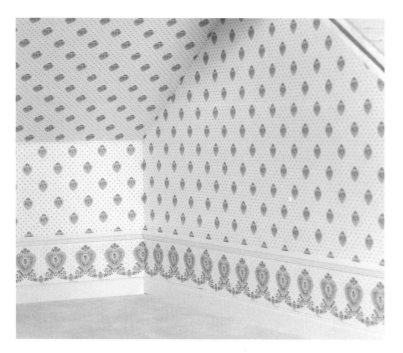

Top: The heart border was used below a wooden chair rail in this room. Bottom: Use wallpaper with an allover pattern in this complicated dormer. Tear-and-tape patterns were made of each wall.

½" back from each corner. Smear the glue with your finger or a wipe out tool so the glue is a thin coat toward the edge of the cardboard. Carefully line up the fabric and pat it in place. Don't pull or stretch the fabric, but make sure the fabric is smooth and even on the face side. Then glue the opposite edge to the back side of the liner, using the same technique. Now glue the remaining edges, always working one edge, then the opposite edge.

There will be excess fabric at all the corners. Working from the back, lay sharp scissors on their side and trim off the dog-ears. You should end up with diagonal cuts into the corner that are still loose from the cardboard. Neatly add some Tacky glue on the corners and smooth the diagonal edges down. You may have a little overlapping, but if it is excessive, trim the fabric a little closer. Glue down any threads that seem to want to stick out. That's usually a neater treatment than attempting to trim them away. Check the face side to see that the fabric has gone smoothly over the corners and that there are no bubbles or wrinkles.

Using this technique for getting rid of the excess material eliminates lumps in the corners when you glue the fabric wall into the dollhouse. Use Tacky glue to put the wall in the house—center wall first, then side walls.

You can use the cardboard-liner technique with wallpaper, too. In fact, when you do a roombox, this is a good way to make a fake back wall or, in some cases, to make angled walls for a more interesting display.

When doing a roombox, use mat board or illustration board that is ⅟₁₆" to ⅛" thick. Walls that aren't glued directly to the sides of the box should be supported with bass stripwood at least ⅛" thick or more. (This is a good way to use up scrap wood.)

You may paste wallpaper directly to the liner on the face side. Cut it so there is excess paper to go around the edge of the liner on the side edges. It's especially important to cover the front edges of the side walls. Otherwise, the cardboard liner leaves an unsightly white line. At the top and bottom of the liner, moldings will cover the cut paper edge.

the fabric ½" to 1" larger than the liner all the way around.

Flip the liner and the fabric over to the wrong sides. Lay the fabric out first with the liner on top of it. Now you'll glue the fabric to the liner, but to the wrong side of the liner to prevent the glue from staining the fabric.

Starting on the edge that needs the fabric pattern to be most even, apply a line of glue about ¼" from the edge of the cardboard, beginning and ending the glue line

When gluing the walls in the roombox, attach the side walls, floor, and ceiling first. This provides a little stop that will support the back wall. Add wood strips for even more support.

In a roombox, pebble-grain white or off-white mat board provides a nice finish for the ceiling. As to the floor, wood flooring can be directly applied to the box floor. Carpeting is more successful when applied to a cardboard liner.

TILE

Individual ceramic tiles and plastic sheet tile may also be used on walls. In the next chapter there is a photograph of a room with sheet tile flagstone on the floor and sheet square tile on the wall. Install the plastic sheet tile the same way as on a floor. Touch up gaps in the wall application with Red Devil's One Time Spackling paste or white paint. Since tile usually needs clamping to stick down in the glue, jam boards or books up against the wall with canned goods or other wedges to hold them in place. Always protect the tile with waxed paper first.

You'll use a different technique for individual ceramic tiles. These are handmade. The ones shown here are made by Ann Shepley of England.

There are two successful ways to install tiles. One is to mount them on a thin cardboard backing and glue that to the wall. The other is to use nylon net as the backing. Either way, you start by making a pattern of the wall. Measure a detailed design for the

Top: The roombox has fabric wallcovering. Bottom: This sample board demonstrates applying glue to the cardboard liner and how to miter the corner dog-ears so fabric lies smooth in the corners.

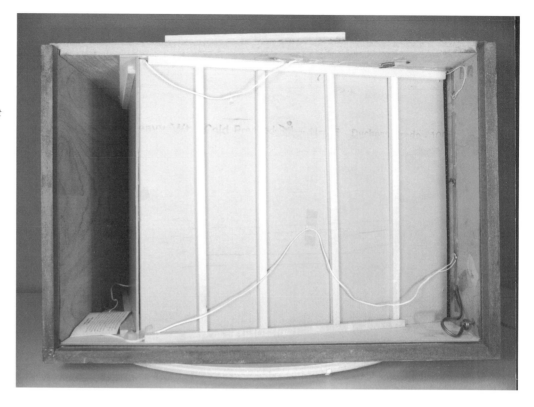

The back of the room-box shows how strip-wood is used to support the walls.

tiles on the pattern. Count and order the number of tiles you need.

The method shown is the one using nylon net. I drew the pattern on grid paper and taped it to the table top. Then I covered it with waxed paper and taped that down, also. Then I taped white nylon net over it. Using Tacky glue and following the pattern, I stuck the tiles to the net, allowing no extra spacing between the tiles, as the tile irregularities provided the minute spacing needed. When tiles had to be cut, I used a tile pliers.

When the glue was dry, I cut out the tile wall with the waxed paper stuck to the netting. This gave extra support to the unit while I was fitting it in the room. Then I re-

moved the waxed paper before permanently installing the tile. When the glue was dry between the tile and the wall, I grouted the tiles with One Time Spackling paste.

Since this is in an extremely narrow bath, I finished the one side wall and the center wall before installing the second side wall—which is a partition—in the body of the house.

WAINSCOTING

If you are going to use the wood of the dollhouse wall as part of wainscoting in a room, you must prepare that wall now. This type of wainscoting was used in the Newport. I marked the dimensions on the wall, primed it, and gave it one coat of paint. After applying wallpaper to the upper half of the wall, I wiped the lower half clean of any excess wallpaper paste. If you don't get the paste off it curdles the paint. Application of the wood trim panels is discussed in Chapter 13, which deals with interior moldings.

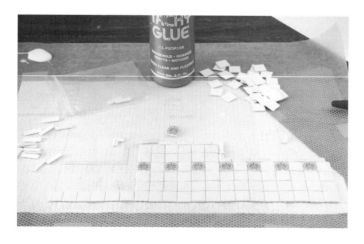

Use Tacky glue to stick the tiles to the nylon net base.

Left: Flowers were cut from the wallpaper and used as the "patterned" pieces in the tile wall. Right: The hearth is inlaid in the printed, textured slate floor.

Remember to check where lighting goes before permanently installing the flooring. You can measure and cut flooring and set it aside until light fixtures are in place. Since bits of debris cling to velveteen carpeting, it's best to postpone installing it until everything else is finished. If it must be installed early on, cover it with a cloth to catch the debris.

Use tracing paper or waxed paper for the template of a floor that is to be used on patterned flooring. Use notebook paper if the flooring has no pattern.

If there are doorways in the rooms, determine if the flooring will need to extend into that area, too. If no component door will fill the opening, you may use a wood strip, especially if the flooring doesn't look quite right in the doorway. For tile floors, the wood strip may be painted a matching color as if it were a marble threshold.

PLASTIC SHEET TILE

This flooring comes in sheets that vary in size. Always take your room dimensions to the store with you when you go to buy it.

All the flooring in this 1/144th scale house is printed paper.

There are three varieties of tile flooring—embossed tile, printed textured tile, and plastic coated, printed card stock. The embossed flooring is a lightweight plastic that has the pattern molded into it. The background is the grout color and the tile color is printed on the raised tile area. Some popular brand names are J.R. Enterprises and Miniature House. J.R. Enterprises flagstone and square tile were used in the Glencroft. In this example, I used tile on the wall. I cut flowers from the wallpaper and applied them to the tile to make it appear as if they were fancy hand-painted tiles.

The printed, textured tile is a heavier plastic, about the thickness of a real vinyl floor tile. The whole piece is textured, but the grout—or in some cases the pattern— is printed on. The manufacturer is Eden Craft. An example of this tile is the slate floor in the Newport.

The printed, plastic coated card stock is usually a linoleum pattern. Craft Products prints some old Armstrong patterns. What's Next prints checkerboard patterns and a colorful Portuguese type tile.

Lay the tracing paper pattern right side up on the right side of the tile. (This means the wrong side of the paper pattern touches the right side of the tile.) Move it around until the design in the tile is centered on the paper pattern. Usually the edge of the floor along the open edge of the dollhouse is aligned with the straight edge of the tile design. Tape the pattern to the tile and cut around the pattern with scissors or a rotary cutter and straightedge.

Try the tile in the dollhouse room. Chances are it will need a little final trimming to lie without buckling. If you must piece the tile, make the seam run side to side in the room and toward the back, so that it's not as noticeable.

When the fit is satisfactory, glue the tile in place using the glue recommended by the manufacturer. Tacky glue is usually their choice. Solvent base glues will mar the vinyl tiles. Use a stickflat glue to lay the plastic coated card flooring.

Lay waxed paper over the tile and weigh it down to dry. With embossed tile, it's important to weight the edges, since they tend to curl up. Put books or boards into the corners and weight them with canned goods.

PAPER FLOORING

Paper flooring is made by J. Hermes and is particularly popular in the smaller scales—

¹/24, ¹/48, or ¹/144. The paper stock it's printed on behaves just like the thinner printed-for-dollhouse wallpaper.

Make a tracing paper pattern of the floor to be covered. Center it on the paper flooring, as if you were doing a tile floor. Test-fit it in the dollhouse room, trimming when necessary. Use Grandma Stover's Stickflat glue or Mini-Graphics Mucilage to stick down the floor. When it's thoroughly dry, coat it with several coats of Ceramacoat's semi-gloss varnish.

CARPETING

The most widely used carpeting in miniatures is upholstery velvet or cotton velveteen. MiniGraphics and B.H. Miniatures package it to coordinate with their wallpapers. You may also find it sold by the yard at your local fabric store. Take your room dimensions and a wallpaper sample with you when you shop for the carpeting. It comes in several sizes, and the nap makes the fabric change shades when it's laid in different directions. This may affect the size of the piece you buy.

With velveteen carpeting, examine the piece and decide which way you want it to lie in the room. Sometimes it's important to have the darker or lighter color showing to better coordinate with wallpaper. Lay the carpeting right side up on your work table with the shading as you want it in the dollhouse. The open edge should be toward you. Now slip the pattern under the carpeting with the right side markings up. Flip the whole unit over and tape the pattern in place. Use a rotary cutter and straightedge to cut around the carpeting. Fit it in your room, trimming edges when necessary. Any notches that must to be cut out are easier to do with sharp scissors.

NOTE: *Because of the pile or nap on velveteen, you can cut it more accurately when the backing side is up.*

The recommended adhesive for carpeting is the stickflat paste you used on the

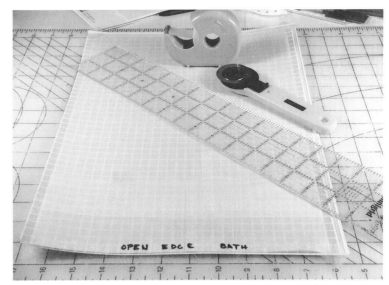

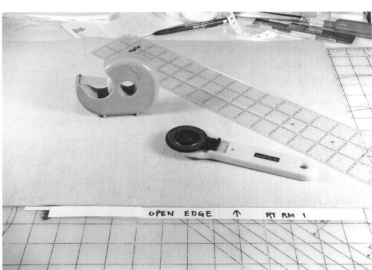

wallpaper. Apply it to the floor, lay the carpeting in place, and pat it smooth. Don't roll or weight the carpeting, as that would flatten the nap. If it is necessary to raise the carpeting later, just dampen the velvet slightly, and it will come up without the nap being pulled away from the back. It's not always necessary to completely cover the floor with glue. In the Twelve Oaks, I laid the carpeting by sticking it down only along the open edge of the house. The baseboard moldings hold it in place along the remaining edges.

When all the wall treatments and flooring are in place, you are ready to install doors and windows.

Top: A see-through tracing paper pattern is centered on the embossed plastic sheet tile. Bottom: Slipping the floor pattern under the velvet carpeting and flipping the two pieces over together ensures getting the pattern on the velvet with the nap in the right direction.

12 INSTALLING THE DOORS AND WINDOWS

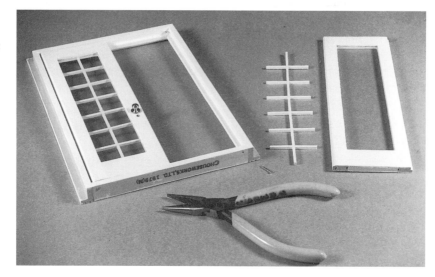

Pull the hinge pin from the threshhold side of the door frame to release the door for painting. The window grid can be popped for finishing. With some doors, the glass slides out a slot, too.

Doors

Doorway openings in dollhouses vary between models because of architectural design and preferences of individual manufacturers. Four styles are shown in this book. The simplest is the partial partition wall with the doorway opening the full floor-to-ceiling height. This is the type of door in the attics of the Heritage and Twelve Oaks and throughout the Cranberry Cove.

The doors in the Glencroft and Heritage models are layered die-cut pieces. The door in the Heritage has pivot hinges as an integral part of the door piece. The doors in the Glencroft have no hinges. If you want them to open and close, you must add the hardware yourself.

The last style shown is a pre-assembled unit containing the framing, threshold, and door. This self-contained component slips into a pre-cut opening in the house. Such doors are featured in the Twelve Oaks and the Newport.

Door knobs and knockers aren't usually included in dollhouse kits. Separate hardware, including in-scale door hinges, are made by Houseworks, Miniature House, Realife, and Clare-Bell Brass. Choose the style that goes best with the architecture of your house.

The easiest way to finish a door unit is to have the door separate from the frame. If the doors for your house are pre-assembled, this means you must pull out the hinge pins and remove the doors from the frame. If the doors for your house are already separate, try them in place and be sure they swing without binding. On the bottom edge of the door use a pencil to write where that door will fit in the house. Usually a numbering system is best. Write the corresponding number on the wall above the doorway in the area that is to be hidden by the door framing when everything is installed.

If the door binds, sand away the offending rub. On most doors the long edge between the hinge pins is rounded front and back. Sometimes this is the problem area. At other times it is one of the other three edges with the square rims. Keep those rims square while sanding away the spot that rubs. It's important to have a freely moving door because if it doesn't move easily, it will shatter with use.

Lay the doors and their frames on waxed paper to paint. Prime and paint them, following the instructions in Chapter 3. Use a ½" flat brush to apply the paint.

When painting the frames, leave the area that will be glued to the walls unpainted. The threshold is usually stained or painted to match the floor, generally brown.

It's not necessary to paint the bottom edge of the door. Paint the top and side edges, since they can usually be seen. When the door fit is tight, painting these edges can cause rubbing. To alleviate this problem, wipe off the paint while it's wet. There will be color left, but not a thick layer of paint.

If the door is an exterior one, you may have a different color on each side. When it is open the spine shows. Paint that the same color as the side showing.

When painting a door with panels, paint the panels first and then the outer framing. This order gives a neater finish.

When the door units are completely dry, reassemble them by pushing the hinge pins back through the frames into the holes in the doors.

When priming, you can save some time by spraying white-pigmented shellac on the doors. Glue the doors upright to a scrap piece of corrugated cardboard, and remember, the bottom of the door doesn't get finished. Use a thin coat of Tacky and place the doors a bit apart so you can spray all

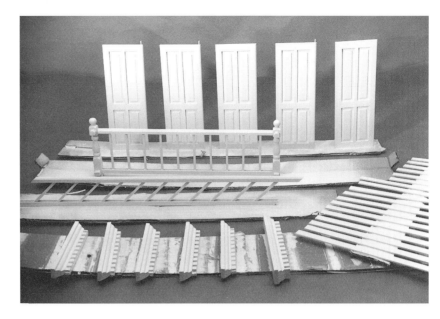

sides at once. If you are painting the threshold, do the same with the door frames. The door frames for the Newport were finished by brush because the threshold was stained to match the floors.

Use Quick Grab glue to install the doorknobs, locks, and knockers as necessary.

Glue the door unit into the house with Tacky glue. Spread a line of glue on the back side of the frame. When pressed in place, the glue will spread and cover the entire back surface.

Pre-assembled interior doors come with the door frame molding for the second side. Exterior doors, including French doors, do not. You have to buy molding for those doors separately and then cut it to fit. Detailed directions for finishing and cutting those moldings is given in the next chapter.

With doors that include moldings, glue the loose frame on the unfinished side. When there is a three-piece molding, place the two sides first and the top trim last. Spread glue on all three pieces before starting to install the molding. Then you will have time to make adjustments before the glue gets too dry. The frame should just cover the crack between the wall and the inside door frame.

The die-cut doors made for this book were finished a little differently. I stained the doors in the Glencroft before cutting the pieces out of the plywood sheets. I covered the main door panel on both sides, the trim panels only on the top side. I assembled the

Various components and trims are "tack" glued to cardboard for easier handling while giving their surfaces a final finish.

The finished front door on the Heritage.

The coat-hanger holding jig for painting non-working pre-assembled windows.

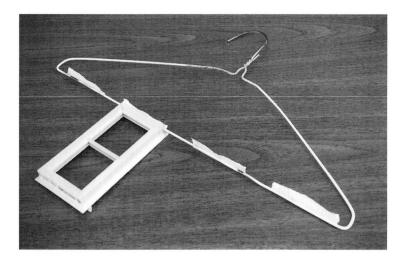

trim that holds the panels in place had to be painted before assembling the door. I glued the door together and held it with clamps until dry. Before installing the framing and door, I had to shape the pivots on the door so they would work easily in the pivot holes in the frame. I did this with craft knife and fingernail file.

Windows

Prepare to paint the windows by laying them on waxed paper. Give them a final finish with either paint or stain. As you assemble windows with clear acrylic panels, remove the protective plastic coverings before permanently installing the windows. But before you begin, read on.

For pre-assembled non-working windows, first remove the clear acrylic panel through the slot in the top. Set the acrylic panel aside in a place where it will not be spattered with paint or scratched accidentally. When painting this style of window, leave the back side of the outer frame free of paint.

This type of window may be primed with spray shellac. Use a wire coat hanger as a holding tool. Tape the window to the hanger, placing the wire through the top of the slot where the acrylic goes.

For pre-assembled working windows, draw lines with a pencil where the sash meets the frame. Do this on both the inside and the outside of the windows. Remove the sashes from the windows. One end of the frame is loose, providing access to the sashes. Slip them out of the frames. One manufacturer requires that you push the window against its spring in the side to remove the sash. Set the springs aside in a safe place.

If you want this kind of window to work after painting, keep the inside of the sash tracks free of paint. On the sashes paint only the area inside the pencil lines. Since this is difficult to do, it's easiest to lay on a stroke of paint and, while it's still wet, wipe off the area that should remain paint-free. This gives a little color without leaving a thick layer of paint. To prevent sticking when the window is reassembled, rub beeswax along the face edges of the sash.

pieces with Tacky glue and held them together with clamps until the glue was dry. Then I gave them a final finish with Ceramacoat varnish.

The front door in the Heritage is a painted door consisting of two parts—main door and exterior trim. Using the trim for the door as a guide, I painted only the visible area on the main piece. This is a clean way to paint contrasting colors on a door. Since this door also has "glass" panels, the

The lower edge of the window frame is loose. Glue it permanently in place after painting the sashes and reinserting them in the frames.

Sometimes a little sanding is necessary, too.

Another area of difficulty is keeping paint off of the acrylic pane. Usually I use an artist's brush with a fine point and paint with no masking. If I miss a stroke, I carefully remove it with my fingernail while the paint is damp-dry.

The preassembled windows used in the Twelve Oaks and the Newport have mullions. These are an extra added detail. Part of the mullions are Bell's plastic ones, but most of them were constructed from 1/16" square wood.

Mullions are not difficult to make, but they are time-consuming. You cut the wood, preferably with a single-edge razor blade, to fit the width and length of each sash. Using grid paper as a guideline, notch the mullions uniformly with the razor so they mesh together flat. Each notch should be to a depth of half the width of the wood. Glue the mullions together and finish them with spray shellac and paint before gluing them in the sashes.

For windows assembled from pre-cut parts, paint the moldings before inserting the acrylic panels. Some styles allow you to partially assemble the windows. Do this assembly when you can, since the paint aids in stabilizing the frame. Recommended glue is Tacky. The moldings for this type of

The Cranberry Cove windows are made from pre-cut parts.

window should be left paint-free on the back side.

After the windows are painted and completely dry, assemble them. Clean the panes if necessary and install them in the frames. Do this very carefully, using liquid anti-static eyeglass cleaner and a soft cleansing tissue or a glass cleaner recommended for acrylic. These panes scratch easily, so use a light touch.

When assembling windows with screen-printed panes, make sure they are right-side up. The sash latch must be on top of the marking. Remove any plastic covering, too.

For die-cut windows, prime or stain the

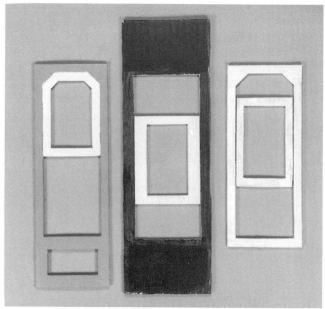

Left, above: The basic window in the Glencroft. Right: The double-hung window in the Heritage.

side that will face outward while the windows are still in the sheets. Carefully remove them from the sheets, keeping the part numbers on the unfinished side of each. Apply a final finish to the inside edges of the windows. The outside edges don't need finishing, as they will be hidden in the house construction.

When making a basic window like that in the Glencroft, glue the screen-printed acetate between the two window pieces. The acetate is printed only on one side, which will have a dull sheen to the printing. This side goes to the outside in all windows. Acetate may be cleaned with eyeglass cleaner.

Since the inside and outside windows are identical, choose the nicest-looking one for the exterior. Glue the acetate pane to the outside window, centering it with the printing facing toward the outside. Use Tacky glue, and when it's dry, glue the inside window to the back of the outside one. Center the inside edges of the window. Any irregularities on the outside edges can be sanded away as you fit the windows into the house.

Chances are you will have to complete the windows before you assemble the body of the house so you can pre-fit them into the openings. As you do this, mark the locations of the windows and the openings on the various parts of the house. Set the windows aside in a safe place until they can be installed in the finished house body.

The windows in the Heritage are working windows. The directions in the kit for putting them together and installing them in the house are comprehensive. They also have acetate sandwiched between inside and outside windows.

On casement windows that open, you'll need to custom-fit the pivot pins by shaping them with craft knife and fingernail file. Some outside edges of the windows must be sanded to fit, too. The outside edges also have to be painted, as they show when the windows are open.

I finished the double-hung windows before adding them to the house. In the photo above, right, on the left is the exterior trim plus top window. In the center is the actual house wall with the outer lower sash, which has to slide easily in the wall. On the right is the inner window trim with the inner lower sash, which has to slide easily within the trim. Once all these parts are final finished and fitted, it's a simple matter to assemble and install the window, following the directions.

Glue the windows on the house using Tacky glue.

Glue the interior window framing or moldings in place, too. Tab-and-slot and tongue-and-groove kits usually provide this molding. If you're using a kit with pre-assembled windows, you'll have to cut the moldings to finish the inside framing. You'll find directions for this procedure in the next chapter.

One window is installed, and the second one is ready to slip the pivot flanges into the holes in the frame. The apron wedges under the sill to hold the windows in place.

13 INTERIOR MOLDINGS

*Left: Priming molding strips with spray shellac.
Right: Painting several strips of molding at one
time with a sash brush.*

The interior moldings for doors, windows, baseboards, cornices, and chair rails can all be given a final finish at the same time. Generally they are all the same color. If you are using several colors, sort the molding pieces according to color. Lay them out on waxed paper.

To make this job go quickly, use the 1½" sash brush and paint several pieces of molding at a time. Hold the moldings so they are barely touching, with the side up that will face the room. The brush bristles will work in between the strips to finish the narrow edges. Leave the back sides paint-free. Sep-

arate the pieces and set them aside to dry. Any warping will disappear as the strips are cut and applied to the walls.

Moldings may also be primed with spray shellac. Attach as many as possible to a wire clothes hanger with bull clip clamps. Using 1½" bull clips, you may get two wood pieces to a clamp. When the shellac is dry, rub down the moldings with a paper bag and proceed with the paint finish. Paint applied by brush seems to give a better finish than spray paint.

When the moldings are thoroughly dry, install them. The order of work is door casing, window casing, baseboards, cornice moldings, and chair rail, if used.

As you cut and install the moldings, touch up the corners and bare ends. A coat of paint generally does the job. If you dip the ends into some paint and wipe the excess off before you install it, that's all the finish that's usually needed. Sometimes you will find it necessary to add a little filler, too. On stained moldings you can sometimes get by using brown marker on the bare wood.

To install the moldings, you will need a hobby miter box and razor saw, Tacky glue, a sharp pointed pencil, and a measuring tape or strip of paper.

Since a hobby miter box and razor saw may be new tools for you, here are a few tips for using it more efficiently.

First of all, when you buy your miter box and saw, get the saw blade that is 1¼" wide by 5½" long and has 54 teeth to the inch. This is the finer blade and makes a nicer cut on basswood moldings. It may be either X-Acto or Pro Edge brand.

If you already have a miter box and saw set, check it to see if the miter box slots have become enlarged and are no longer accurate. If it is in this condition, buy a new box. Cutting molding in the old box will make sloppy miters. Likewise, the saw blade should be sharp. If it isn't, you will have fuzzy cuts that will need additional attention to make them clean. The blade is replaceable, so it's not necessary to buy a handle, too.

Line the bed of the miter box with a piece of scrap wood. Cut the wood to cover the bed fully. The kind that will last longest is a ¹⁄₁₆" thick piece of hobby plywood. This protects the saw blade from quickly becoming dull.

When you use the miter box, place it on the edge of the work table so the lip on the bottom of the box catches on the edge of the table. This will stabilize the box when you are sawing.

Always place the wood you are cutting against the back of the box, with the square edge of the wood firmly against the bed and back sides.

If you aren't used to the action of a hobby saw, it may be a little awkward at first. The secret is to guide the saw back and forth without bearing down on it. Let the tool do the work.

DOOR FRAMING OR SURROUNDS

The basic function of window or door casing is to hide the crack between the wall opening and the window or door framing. The ideal casing fit covers both the crack and the outside edge of the inside framing.

Most exterior and interior doors have their own casings. They come with the preassembled interior door and are usually included with build-it-yourself doors. You have probably already installed them when you put in the door unit.

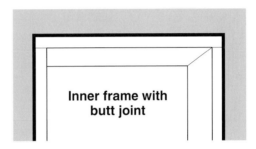

Inner frame with butt joint

For doorways without doors, use ¹⁄₁₆" stripwood the width of the wall for the inside framing. Measure and cut the piece for the top (head) first. Glue it in place. Measure and cut the two side (jamb) pieces. Use straight cuts and butt the corners.

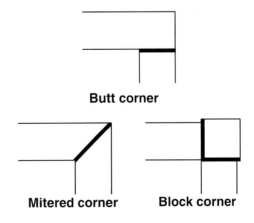

Butt corner

Mitered corner   **Block corner**

The common corner finishes for casings are the butt finish, the mitered corner, and the corner block. Follow the style of moldings that are already in the house, or use a butt finish. Use the following directions for preassembled doors without inside casings as well.

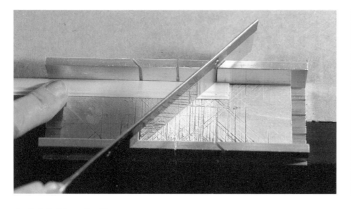

Left: Making the first cut on the headpiece of the door surround. Right: Trimming away a waste triangle.

A butt corner framing is always made from plain, ¹⁄₁₆" stripwood, ³⁄₈" or ½" wide. Measure the opening width and add twice the width of the molding and subtract a smidgen so the jamb moldings will cover the crack.

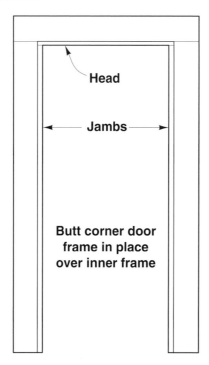

Butt corner door frame in place over inner frame

Cut a top piece to this measurement and tape it in place over the doorway. Measure and cut the two side pieces. Before gluing the top piece permanently in place, be sure its ends are smooth and touched up with paint. Glue the casing around the door, sides first and then top. Repeat for the other side of the wall.

Here's a refinement that can be added to the butt-finish frame. Place a painted piece of ¹⁄₈" x ¹⁄₁₆" stripwood along the bottom edge of the head trim, between it and the jamb casings. Cut this strip ¹⁄₁₆" longer on both ends.

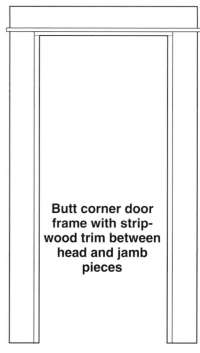

Butt corner door frame with strip-wood trim between head and jamb pieces

Stripwood or a shaped casing molding may also be used for a mitered corner framing. Simply measure the opening and subtract just a smidgen so the side pieces will hide the crack.

Most shaped casing moldings are asymmetrical. They have a thick edge and a thin edge. As you cut your casing, just remember that the thin edge always goes toward the opening.

Cut the top piece first. Place the molding stock in the miter box with the thick edge against the back of the box. Using the 45-degree slot that runs right to left cut off a small piece of molding. This is scrap.

Along the thin edge of the molding, measure the door opening minus a smidgen and mark that edge with a pencil.

Replace the molding in the box with the thin edge against the back. Line up the pencil mark with the 45-degree slot that runs

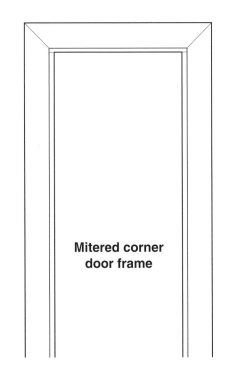

Mitered corner door frame

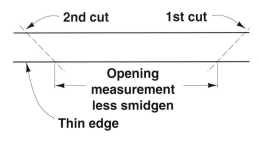

2nd cut   1st cut

Opening
measurement
less smidgen
Thin edge

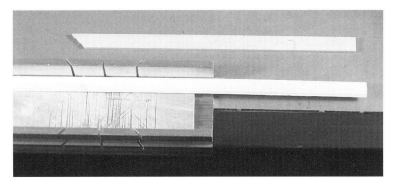

Cutting the second doorjamb.

left-to-right angled slot. Cut the piece. This way of cutting a door casing uses the minimum amount of molding and cutting.

The block corner uses straight cuts throughout. The casing pieces are cut to the measurements of the opening minus a bit to cover the crack. A square piece of wood fills the corner. This square is usually a little wider than the casing stock and may have a bull's-eye circle or be plain. The plain square usually has beveled edges. The casing molding may be shaped, and usually has a symmetrical pattern.

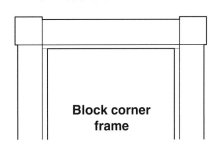

Block corner frame

left to right. Cut the second miter. Tape the piece over the doorway. Now measure the opening for the left side from the inside corner of the top casing piece to the floor along the wall opening—not the inside framing.

The cut on your molding stock is a left-to-right cut, and you need a right-to-left cut. Put the stock in the miter box so the right-to-left 45-degree slot can be used to trim off the scrap wood. Using the left side measurement, mark the thin side of the molding with a pencil. This time the cut will be a straight one. Line up the mark on the molding with the straight slot in the miter box and cut it.

Check the piece for fit, then flip it over and try it on the right side of the door opening. If it fits, use it to mark out the measurement on the molding stock. This time, start the measurement from the straight edge and put a pencil mark on the thin edge of the stock. Line up the mark with the thin edge against the back of the box and in the

WINDOW CASINGS OR SURROUNDS

Window casings follow the same general design as the door casings except for a bottom edge to finish—the sill and apron. As a rule, window casings use the same top corners as the doors in a house. The bottom corners should have a butt joint to be realistic. The side pieces always rest on the bottom board.

Some preassembled windows come with interior trim that has all four corners mitered, but this is rare on real houses. With these windows you can cut off the bottom miters on the side pieces, making a straight edge. Then cut stripwood to replace the bottom piece.

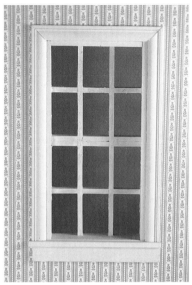

A finished mitered corner window casing with sill.

The window trim should include a sill, especially if the windows are left undressed. This is made of 1/16" stripwood. With some windows, it only needs to be wide enough to glue to the wall, extending an existing sill surface in the window unit. It should be 1/16" wider than the apron board. With other windows, a piece must be wide enough to go from the sash and extend beyond the apron. Cut notches out of each end of the board to fit the wall.

A sill board extends 1/16" beyond the jamb trims. The jamb trim rests on the sill and the apron board fits snugly under the sill.

For maximum support to curtain rods that install into holes in the window frame, use a butt corner. Simple butt framing is the logical choice for windows covered with cornices, too.

BASEBOARDS OR SKIRTING BOARDS

Stripwood, asymmetrical casing moldings, or specially designed baseboard molding can be used to hide the seam between floor and wall. It may be the same throughout the house, or you can use fancy moldings in the public rooms and plainer styles in the utilitarian rooms. The latter custom was prevalent in earlier times. The former method would be contemporary. If stripwood is used throughout, it could indicate a house located in a community where fancy moldings were expensive or unavailable. It's a detail that tells some of the story of who inhabits your dollhouse.

When fitting the baseboard into the house, first fit the baseboard on the center wall or the wall farthest into the room from the open side. Then do the side walls. Always measure for wall moldings along the exact space the molding will cover. There can be fractional differences from top to bottom on the same wall, which will affect the fit of the molding. Leave a staircase wall until you are installing the stairs.

To cut it in the miter box, place baseboard molding on edge with the wide flat width against the back of the box.

The correct corner fit is a butt joint on the inside corners and a mitered joint on the outside ones. This is easy to do with plain stripwood.

Creating a butt corner with a shaped molding requires contouring. Cut the center wall molding the full width of the wall, with straight cuts on both ends. Trim the back edges of the side wall pieces to fit.

Cut a second piece from the stock about 1/2" longer than necessary for the side wall. On the wrong side of this piece, along the edge that will be to the back wall, trace the pattern of the molding, using a piece of scrap as a guide. Use the L-shaped block or a corner jig to hold the pieces so you can mark the wood.

Below, left: Cutting a baseboard in the miter box. Right, top: Trace the contour of the molding on the flat back side of the piece to be shaped. Right, below: The inside and outside corners in baseboard around a chimney breast.

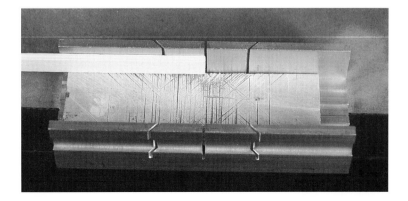

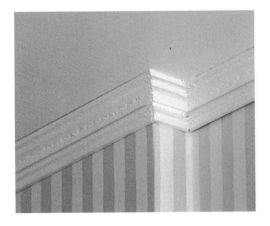

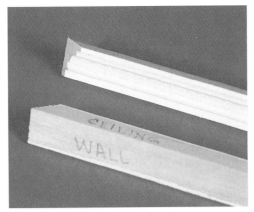

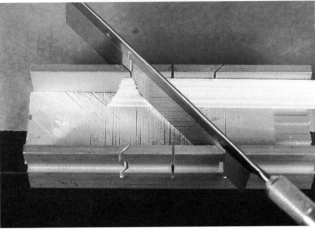

Far left: The inside and outside corners of crown molding around a chimney breast. Left, above: Mark the wrong sides of the crown molding, indicating which is wall and which is ceiling. Left, below: Crown molding is always cut with the ceiling side down against the bottom of the miter box.

First, place the back end of the side wall piece into the corner with the wrong side out. Lay the scrap piece against it with the shaped part out. Hold firmly and trace the contour with a fine-pointed pencil. Carve away the waste with an X-Acto knife. Now fit the side wall piece in the house against the back and mark the front edge for its finish cut. Repeat for the second side.

Outside corners occur most frequently around chimney breasts or in L-shaped rooms. When cutting the piece to fit this type of wall, fit the opposite end first. Cut the piece long, slip it into place, and mark where you have to make the miter cut. The wrong side of the molding will always be shorter. Cut it and glue it into place. Repeat for the second piece.

CORNICE MOLDINGS

The cornice hides the seam between the walls and ceiling in a room. It may be simple or elaborate and is installed with mitered corners. The exception is stripwood which uses a butt corner. Stripwood or cove molding are the simplest finishes. At its most elaborate, a cornice may be composed of several moldings and appear massive and overwhelming. Again, it helps set the mood for a room.

Cove molding is symmetrical, so you will find the ceiling and wall back sides will have an equal measurement, but the other shaped styles are not—one side is always deeper than the other. The deeper side usu-ally goes against the wall and the shallow side against the ceiling. Whichever way you decide to use the molding, be consistent. To keep from confusing ceiling and wall sides, mark the wrong side in pencil several times along its length. Always check this while you're cutting.

As with the baseboards, fit the cornice trim the same way, center wall and then the sides. Measure at the ceiling level to determine the size to cut the cornice stock.

On a mitered cornice, the cut that goes against the ceiling is angled and the wall side is a straight cut. When cutting the cornice in the miter box, the ceiling side of the trim goes on the floor of the box and the wall side goes against the back. A right-to-left cut in miter box becomes the left end of the trim when it's turned into position. Likewise, a left-to-right cut becomes the right end of the molding when turned upright. Cut the back wall molding and tape it in place in the room. Cut the scrap triangle off the molding stock. Place the stock on the appropriate side wall and slide the mitered end into the corner. At the open

Frieze molding and chair railing are used in this dining room.

wood wainscoting or paneling, the heavier substance is always at the bottom.

Determine what dimension you will use and draw a line around the room at that height. To get the mark even, tape a pencil to the appropriate size block of wood or small box and mark around the room.

Chair rail is installed in the same order as cornice molding—first the center wall, then the sides. Strip stock has corner butt joints, while shaped stock uses a contour or a miter joint. When the railing encounters windows and doors, cut it straight and butt it against the framings.

Frieze molding is installed in the same way, only it runs about an inch below the ceiling. It usually is the framing for a border that has been put on the wall under the cornice molding. Sometimes it is used as picture railing. All the pictures in the room are hung from this strip of wood. I used it in the dining room of the Twelve Oaks because the wallpaper fell short of the ceiling.

Other uses of railing can also be functional parts of a room. Plain stock hung with pegs can be used in a Shaker room. Some shops or pubs have plate rails around the top of the wall to display merchandise or collections.

edge of the house, mark the cornice molding. Finish this end of the molding with a straight cut. Make sure it fits the space, and before you glue it into place, finish the end to match the molding.

You can also contour-cut cornice molding as you did the baseboard. Since the cornice is thicker and more intricate in design, contouring takes longer, but gives a satisfying result. As with the baseboard, always use a mitered cut on outside corners.

Cut the rest of the cornice and glue it into place. The exception is a staircase wall. Wait until you are installing the stairs to cut and glue those cornices.

CHAIR RAILING AND OTHER OPTIONAL TRIMS

In most dollhouses, chair railing is an added touch. Originally chair rail was used in rooms where furniture, especially chairs, were frequently pushed against the wall. To preserve the decor, a strip of wood was put up as a stop. Given the reason for chair railing, you'll want to put your chair rail up at a height that is functional in the room—usually somewhere between 2½" and 4" from the floor.

Chair railing may be used to delineate between two coordinating wallpapers, as in the Twelve Oaks. Sometimes it separates wallpaper on top and paint on the bottom, or vice versa. When using tile, linoleum, or

WAINSCOTING PANELS

I used a very simple wood wainscoting in the Newport. I primed and painted the wooden walls with one coat of acrylic paint, then primed and painted double bead molding and cut it into pieces to make a rectangular pattern on the wall.

To set up the pattern, I first measured the side walls in the dining room and parlor of the house. On ¼" grid paper, I measured an area this length by 2½" high. I marked the width of the baseboard along the bottom of the wainscoting and added the width of the chair rail to the top edge of the wainscoting, thereby making the area 2¾" high.

Since corner posts were visible in Colonial houses, I installed ⅛" x ⅛" corner posts

Wainscoting in the Newport's parlor.

in the corners of the room. The open edge of the wall has a piece of stripwood ¼" x ¹⁄₁₆" as a stop. These pieces were also added to the pattern. The corner and edge pieces made it possible to use straight cuts when cutting the chair railing and baseboard moldings. The only mitering I had to do was on the outside corners of the chimney breasts.

With the boundaries set, the remaining space was evenly divided. I decided on one-half inch spacing between the panels and one quarter inch spacing between top and chair rail and bottom and baseboard.

Once the size of the panels was set, I marked the measurements of the long and the short side on the edge of the pattern and used this as a gauge to cut the pieces from the molding.

I miter-cut the double bead molding with a miter tool. This tool is not a "must have," but it is extremely useful for this job. Its idiosyncrasy is that it pushes the

wood grain down along the edge it cuts. This makes a dented miter if all the pieces are cut from the front side of the molding. To compensate for this effect, you must cut one side of the miter from the front of the molding and the second side of the miter from the back side.

In the course of cutting all these framing pieces, I discovered that if I always held the molding against the left guide on the tool with the excess wood always pointed toward the left, the miter cuts automatically went

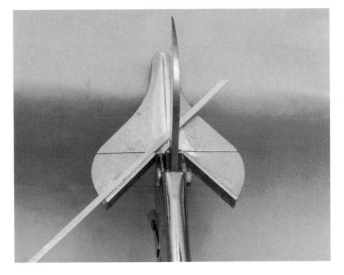

This is the correct way to hold molding in the miter tool for cutting—for a right-handed person. The position should be reversed for a left-handed person.

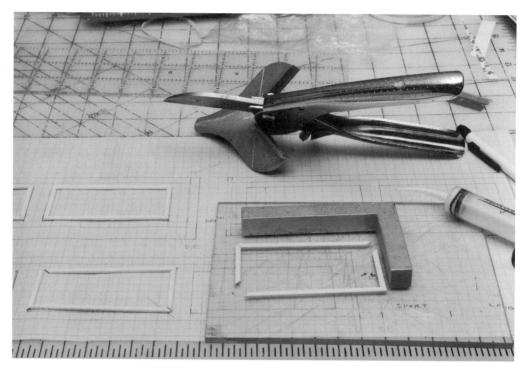

Gluing the molding into rectangles by using the L-square to keep the sides square.

Below: The spacer lies on top of the stairs.

first from the front side and second from the back side.

After cutting the pieces, I glued the panel frames together with Tacky. Pushing the corners into an L-square kept them true. First I glued two sets of a long and a short piece, then glued these pairs together, forming a frame.

When all the frames for a room were made, I glued them onto the house wall. I made spacers of scrap ½" and ¼" wood and laid them on top of the baseboard and between the panels as I put the frames in place. It's easier to use spacers than to try to measure and mark the walls with pencil.

The end walls in each room were different sizes because of the chimney breasts. Each panel frame had a different width. Because of the small space, I used a ¼" spacer.

The lower floor staircase wall needed framed panels, too. I maintained the same height as on the straight wall. However, I had to cut new angles to give the panels their correct miter.

I used a piece of ⅛" stripwood as a spacer between the stair treads and the framing. Between the panel and the chair rail is ¼" spacing. I marked lines on the wall, setting up the pattern, and traced the two new angles onto paper. Working on the paper as shown in the diagram, I bisected the angles, providing the new miter angles. Then I cut them with a single-edge razor blade and laid the wood on the pattern, lining it up with one arm of the angle. I made the cut by lining up the razor blade with the other arm. Each piece of framing will have one angle on one end and the other angle on the other end.

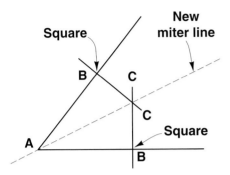

To create your diagram for new miter angles, follow these steps: Measure an equal distance from the point of the angle down each arm, AB. At point B, draw lines toward the middle, making sure that lines BC are perpendicular or square to lines AB. Draw a line from point A through the intersection of lines BC. This is the new miter line. Do this for both acute and obtuse angles.

There are other styles of wainscoting. If you are interested in doing something more complicated, look in architectural books for ideas. If you live near a historical home with wainscoting, go there to study the design.

When you've installed all the moldings in a room, you're ready to install the chandeliers or any dangling light fixtures. There should be no further reason to turn the house upside-down during in construction.

14 EXTERIOR TRIMS

When adding the finishing trim to the house, work from the body of the house outward. Add the shutters and any trim that goes on the house shell first. Then add secondary trim like gingerbread in the apex of gables and corbels under the eaves. Install porch railings and trims. Add the front steps if they are a separate unit.

On the open side of the house, add stripwood trim to the open edges. This gives a finished look to the edges of partitions and the house if they aren't particularly smooth.

Finally, if your house has no cover for the open side, add a track to hold a clear acrylic or glass panel that will protect the contents from dust.

Give all the pieces of exterior trim a final finish before adding it to the house. It's easier to paint them when they are flat on your work table.

SHUTTERS

Originally, in real life, shutters had a vital function. They kept the cold and bad weather out of the house. The first shutters were boards nailed to crosspieces that latched to the house. Then, as woodworking skills improved and styles changed, the paneled kind, such as those used on the Newport, became popular. I installed these shutters to give the illusion of functioning shutters. They are glued in place with the edge of the shutter at the inside edge of the frame, as if it could be closed. The black shutter holdbacks were used on real houses to hold the shutters open in good weather.

The louvered shutters on the Twelve Oaks are decorative and nonfunctional. They are glued to the house with the louvers down so the rain will run off instead of into the house wall. If

The paneled shutters on the Newport, with black wrought-iron holdbacks.

Decorative louvered shutters on the Twelve Oaks.

you want the shutters to appear as if they worked, install them with the louvers up, so when they are closed against the weather the rain would run off instead of in. You should also put the edge of the shutter at the inside edge of the window frame instead of the outside edge as on the Twelve Oaks.

When finishing shutters, do them all at the same time. Use a holding jig to make the job easier. Cut a strip of stiff cardboard 2" wide and long enough to hold all the shutters. Space them a little apart, so that you can easily paint the side edges. Use a few lines of glue to hold the back of the shutters to the board. Now you have a way to hold the shutters so all the sides can be painted at once. The holding jig also makes it possible to spray them with shellac. After rubbing them down with a brown paper bag, give them their final paint finish. Use a big brush to distribute the paint and a smaller one to pull excess amounts out of the crevices.

PORCH POSTS AND RAILINGS

At this point in their construction, you can put the front porch in place on almost all dollhouses. Sometimes the pillars or posts are there too, if only as a temporary support for the porch roof. Kit directions will give specifics for installing the railings and trims. There are usually good instructions for spacing the posts to take the railings.

Generally, it's better to paint the components to a porch railing and then assemble it afterward with Tacky glue. Use holding jigs for the parts, and glue the ends of the spindles to a piece of cardboard along with the ends of the hand rail. Spray them with

Use a jig to evenly space the spindles in a porch railing.

shellac. Rub them down with a paper bag and brush on the remaining coats of paint. Sometimes even spray paint may be used, especially on the spindles.

The Twelve Oaks kit had a jig included for spacing the spindles in the porch railing. The jig makes it very easy to space them evenly and glue them in a perpendicular position.

When I glued the porch railing units in place, I used extra spindles to space the railings off the floor. This allows for the rain to run off the porch. I didn't use this spacing on the Cranberry Cove (the house for a child) because I felt the railing would be fastened more securely for playing if the bottom edge was glued to the floor.

TRIM STRIPS, GINGERBREAD, AND FASCIA BOARDS

Trim strips are plain pieces of wood that have been painted, usually the same color as the house, and are glued in place wherever needed to give the house a finished look. I used them in the end gables of the Twelve Oaks, at the eave line, and where the extension intersects the house. They hide the seams. I added additional strips to the edge of the roof pieces all the way around.

On the Heritage, the gingerbread apex trim in the gables and dormer hides the seam between the wall and the roof. The fascia board on the edge of the roof hides the seam between gingerbread trim and the roof.

Install any trims put on the edges of the roof after the back roof section is in place. Since you can make these

Right, above: Use two spindles as spacers when realistically installing porch railing. Below: For practicality's sake, the railing is glued directly to the porch floor on this child's dollhouse.

boards the same color as other trims on the house, it's convenient to paint them all at one time now.

On the Newport, the frieze pieces cover the seam between house and roof. Sometimes you can give the architecture still more trim by mounting corbels on top of the frieze.

All these trims are basically a form of stripwood. They may be finished as if they were moldings—done en masse. Follow the specific directions given in your kit for placing them.

BACK EDGE FINISHING

If you painted the back edges of your house when you constructed the body, you may not need to add any stripwood finish. However, if the edges are still rough, you may want to add the stripwood anyway. Be sure to consider whether or not adding the stripwood will interfere with an acrylic cover.

The back edges in the Heritage kit are already finished—the support posts are on the body of the house, and the partitions have a small edge trim. Dura-craft kits usually include this nicely, so they are ready to have a track attached for the acrylic cover.

The Glencroft has such thin walls, it's difficult to add stripwood to them. Since the walls are so thin, the edges are not noticeable, so I left them with just a paint finish.

The Twelve Oaks had good grade plywood in the house body that finished very well. I didn't add stripwood to the back edges. I finished the Newport's front edges the same way. If it had been desirable to add stripwood to the edges, I would have done it before fitting the front walls and adding the hinges. The stripwood would affect the operation of the front walls if they were added after the hinges were installed.

In contrast, because the edge of the partitions were finished with stripwood in the

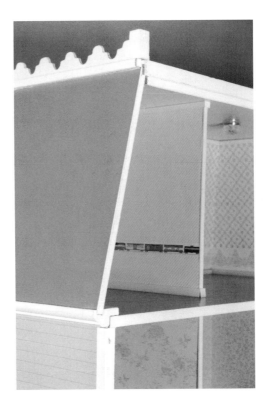

The back edges of the Cranberry Cove are finished with stripwood.

Cranberry Cove, so were the back edges of the house. The stripwood I used is slightly wider than the plywood walls. This helps prevent little fingers from picking the wallpaper loose.

If you decide to use a stripwood edging, measure the house for how much wood you will need. Bass stripwood comes in 24" lengths. Use the $1/32$" or $1/16$" thickness by whatever width the plywood edges are. Usually they are $1/4$" to $3/8$" thick. Prepare the strips as you did your other moldings. It's best to match the color to the house trim or to the woodwork in the rooms. Use a neutral color for the strips—usually white or off-white—so the edges are not more eye-catching than the things displayed in the house. Measure and cut the pieces needed and glue them in place with Tacky. If you don't get all the excess glue off, don't worry—the Tacky dries clear.

15 INSTALLING THE BACK ROOF AND ACRYLIC PANEL TRACK

If you haven't prepared the back roof pieces, do it now, following the directions given for the front roof. Prime the interior, apply a final finish to the eaves, and have the grid for shingles in place. If you can't see the ceiling area of this section, paint it white. That helps reflect light back into the room.

While the roof is still flat on the work table, attach the track for an acrylic cover. That applies only if your back roof has a viewing opening in it, and you must attach the back roof to the house before installing the clear back cover. Attach any remaining fascia or roof trim boards, and then the apex trims or corbels, if you are using them.

Chances are you have never seen an acrylic cover for a dollhouse. They are not in kits and are usually a custom item. They aren't difficult to make and add immensely to the enjoyment of your dollhouse. The things inside don't collect dust, and you can see the house without having to remove sheets or other covers. All the houses in the book have acrylic covers except the Newport, which has a protective front wall.

TRACK FOR THE ACRYLIC PANEL

The easiest cover to make is the one for the Cranberry Cove. The house has a flat back with a mansard roof. I made track for the bottom and top edges of the dollhouse to hold the panel in place. I can slide the acrylic panel in from the side, or slide it all the way up into the top track, then drop it into the lower track. I cut the cover with slanted corners to match the silhouette of the house.

The back of the Glencroft is similar to the Cranberry Cove. It has a flat back. I added a small piece of wood in each top corner to hold the acrylic panel against the house and attached a track to

The track for the acrylic cover on the Glencroft is made from spruce strip-wood, $1/8$" x $1/8$" for the spacer and $1/8$" x $1/2$" for the lip.

the lower edge. Because of the side roof extensions, the acrylic cover can be inserted only by sliding the cover up under the wooden stops and dropping it into the bottom track. This house cover, too, needed a shaped top to fit the contours of the house.

The back sides of the Heritage and the Twelve Oaks offer a complication. Their back roofs are slanted and have openings for viewing the top floor. An acrylic cover slides right out of the track unless you use some mechanical means to hold it in place. Hence, I had to invent a cover latch.

Your dollhouse kit is going to be similar to one of the kits used in this book. Take these general directions and adjust them for your house.

The clear acrylic sheets used for the houses in this book are replacement panels for storm doors. You can get them at a discount house or building center. They are medium strength, 3/32" thick. That means the spacer in the panel track can be 1/8" or a little wider.

The track for the lower edge of the house is spruce stripwood, which is available from the hobby shop in a limited selection of sizes. All pieces are 36" long. I used the 1/8" x 1/8" for the spacer and the 1/8" x 1/2" for the lip strip. Glue one piece of each size together with one edge flush, using carpenter's glue. Clamp them for a strong bond.

Treating this as a unit, cut it to fit the lower edge of the house. Spread glue along the 1/8" spacer to attach it to the house.

I made the upper edge track on the Cranberry Cove of 1/8" x 1/8" and 1/8" x 1/2" stock. Since the roof plywood was only 1/4" thick and didn't provide enough backing for the track, I glued a piece of 1/8" x 1/2" stock on edge to the ceiling of the top rooms to give support to the acrylic panel.

On houses with roofs that slant down over the upper edges of the panels, there's frequently enough support between the roof and the side edge of the house so no other track is needed. In cases where the panel gaps from the house, a piece of scrap wood glued to the eave will serve as the track and keep the panel against the house.

The track for the back roof with a cutout area requires some planning. The roof on the Twelve Oaks is easy to work with and provides a good prototype. That roof has an opening with squared corners. The wood in the piece is 3/8" thick.

The track on the Heritage is made from 1/8" x 1/8" spruce for the spacer and all-purpose trim board from the kit for the lip.

This is the latch for the ³⁄₈" roof, made from a bamboo skewer.

Make a track for the opening with two pieces of ¹⁄₈" x ¹⁄₈" wood. Cut it to fit the three sides of the opening with a butt joint in the corners. Glue the two pieces in place with the one piece flush with the inside edge of the roof and the other flush with the outside edge. Keep a ¹⁄₈" space in the middle.

Since the acrylic panel needs a latch to hold it in place, you can make one using the bottom edge of the roof as the base. You need two pieces of ¹⁄₈" x ¹⁄₈", one piece of ¹⁄₁₆" x ³⁄₈" basswood, and a bamboo skewer from the grocery store to make the latch. The skewer is slightly less than ¹⁄₈" in diameter and very strong.

Cut the two pieces of ¹⁄₈ x ¹⁄₈" and the ¹⁄₁₆ x ³⁄₈" wood to the length of the bottom edge of the roof. Glue the two ¹⁄₈ x ¹⁄₈" pieces in place just as you did in the roof opening. Spread glue on the ¹⁄₈" surfaces of the track and place the ³⁄₈" stripwood on it. Use masking tape to clamp it in place until the glue is dry.

Slide the skewer into the hole created and size it for your roof. Cut it so the skewer is the length of the bottom edge of the roof plus the thickness of the opening track and the fascia board on the side of the roof.

The Heritage roof also needed a cover track and latch. Here the roof wood is only ¹⁄₈" thick, and the third floor of the house protrudes the thickness of the roof wood. The cover has to lie on top of the roof piece to work.

The roofing in this kit is redwood shingles and there are some spare redwood fascia trim boards. I used these on the face side of the track to match the roof color. The fascia board is ³⁄₃₂ x ⁵⁄₁₆".

The roof opening on this house had rounded corners. I cut it out so the corners were square. I made the track by gluing ¹⁄₈ x ¹⁄₈" stripwood to the fascia board with the edges flush. I cut this to fit only the two sides of the opening because I was running out of fascia board. I glued the track in place with the open edge flush with the edge of the roof. The roof is the second side of the cover track.

The latch is very simple. I drilled a hole the diameter of a ³⁄₄" brad in the ¹⁄₈" spacer about ¹⁄₈" from the bottom edge and inserted the brad from the roofing side inward. I dulled the pointed tip of the brad with a hammer.

THE CLEAR ACRYLIC COVER

Once the tracks are installed it's time to fit the acrylic cover. Glass can be substituted and works well on small projects, but when

Left: The track on the Heritage is made from redwood strips that match the roof shingles. Above: The latch on the Heritage is a brad that slides through a hole in the spacer.

a large sheet must be used, clear acrylic is the better choice since it is lighter in weight. Acrylic is definitely the choice for a child's dollhouse.

You can use several tools to cut sheet acrylic. An acrylic cutter is the hand tool most professionals use, and it's inexpensive to buy. It has a hooked end with a V chisel shape to it. You use it like a utility knife. Work on a protected table top, as you would with a rotary cutter. Use a straightedge to guide the cutter and pull toward yourself. Score the acrylic with repeated strokes until the groove or cut is about halfway through the sheet. At that point, lay the cut along the edge of the table and snap the acrylic at the groove to break it along the cut. Sand away any roughness.

The second way to cut sheet acrylic is to use a scroll saw. This tool is very helpful with a cut other than a straight line. Run the saw at a fairly low speed, so the acrylic doesn't melt as you cut. Always make a test cut before sawing into the project.

Sheet acrylic always comes with protective coatings on both sides. It's usually a clear plastic film that may be colored pink or blue. Once in a while it's brown paper with a peel-away adhesive. Leave the coatings on the acrylic until all the cutting is done. This protects the surface from scratches. You can also mark your intended cuts on the protective coating with a pen. This coating also keeps the acrylic from melting during cutting.

If you don't want to cut the acrylic panels yourself, a glass shop will do it for you. Take a pattern or the dimensions of what you want cut to them. Specify the $3/32"$ thickness of the acrylic.

There are two ways to measure your house for the acrylic cover—with a tape measure or a posterboard pattern. When using a tape measure, take measurements for the width of the house at the top, middle, and bottom of the area to be covered. Measure the height at both sides. Transfer the measurements to the sheet of acrylic.

For a house with a shaped silhouette, like the Glencroft or Cranberry Cove, make a posterboard pattern just as you did for the flooring—cutting and taping pieces in place. On the Cranberry Cove I traced the roof line onto the posterboard and cut to fit. I did the same thing with the Glencroft, as the two side roofs that make the top line irregular are a straight angle to the posterboard. To make the piece fit, I cut the board short of the pencil tracings. If you happen to trim too much off the pattern, tape posterboard to the pattern to make it fit.

If the shape is crucial, as with the Glencroft, trace the pattern onto corrugated cardboard the same thickness as the acrylic panel. Fit this first. Then trace and cut the acrylic. Make your cutting lines just inside the pen markings.

Because of the drop in the roof line on the Twelve Oaks, I made the back cover in three pieces—a center section and pieces for the two extensions. The track at the bottom edge is all one.

Because the Twelve Oaks has very shallow eaves, I made the measurement of the back panels equal to the distance from the bottom of the track to the intersection of the eaves and the house. The panels covering the wings of the house slide in from the sides. To slip the center panel into place, I gently bow the acrylic.

16 SHINGLING

The grid on the gable illustrates how to work from the center to the edge of an area that must be shingled.

At this point, all the roof pieces are in place. You have installed track for an acrylic cover if you wanted it. It's a good idea to put the cover in place while installing the shingles to protect the flooring from bits of roofing. If you aren't using a cover, protect the flooring with drop cloths.

The house roof should be marked with the grid for spacing the shingles. On a symmetrical roof, mark the center line from eaves to peak. The center line is your guide for setting up the shingle pattern. You will always alternate rows. In one row, center the

shingle on the line; in the other, put the slit between shingles at the center line. Always work from the center out. If there is any discrepancy in the size of the shingles it will not show as much as it does when you start at the edge of the roof.

On an irregular roof like the one on the Heritage, start the shingle pattern at the edge. Always work the main roof first. This is the one with its full surface usually facing square to the front.

Since there was a dormer in that roof, I applied the shingles only on the roof area

The row of shingles above the dormer are taped in place so the correct pattern for them can be set up in the space to the left of the dormer.

The bevel gauge lying on top of the shingles is set up with the current angle for trimming shingles that butt the roof valley.

to the right of the dormer until I reached its peak. I taped the next row in place and drew a center line down to the edge of the eaves. I marked X's on the rows that would have the same pattern as the taped one and applied shingles to the area left of the dormer until they lined up with the right side rows. Then I could complete the roof without having to finagle shingles to make them fit.

The question of applying flashing to a dollhouse roof sometimes comes up. On an architecturally correct house it would be used. You can use pieces of copper sheeting in the valleys of the roof, glued in place with Quick Grab. Another way to simulate flashing is with paint. Metallic copper is available in acrylic or model paint. Apply a couple of coats in the joint areas. Since real copper flashing normally oxidizes and turns green, you can get a realistic effect on yours by coloring it with a paint wash or by using an oxidizing chemical on the copper.

You may also simulate joints between the roof and chimney. Use a picture of a chimney-roof joint as a guide for placing your flashing. Flashing may also be black, simulating tarpaper or other materials used for roof lining.

After the roofing is completed, trim it out of the valley junction between the roofs. This leaves a little trench with the flashing showing through.

You can take artistic license with the flashing and pretend it's not there. In real life, it's not very noticeable from the ground. Consequently, the samples in this book were done without flashing. Instead I trimmed the shingles so they met closely when matched in the roof valleys.

To make a neat valley on a roof using trimmed shingles, cut an accurate angle on the shingle with its edge lying in the seam.

Shingling the roof of the Glencroft.

Use a bevel gauge or a file card to duplicate the angle. Line up one edge with the valley seam and draw a line on the card at the grid line. If you are using a bevel gauge, line up the second edge with the grid line and tighten the holding screw to keep the angle. Then, holding the shingle on the angle duplicator, mark the shingle. Cut the excess off using a miter cutter or knife.

Always do the main roof first, then the dormers and gables. That way the secondary roof shingles will lie on top of the main roof ones. If your shingles are thick, you may find you have to use a steeper angle on the secondary shingles or else notch them out. Always check or make a new pattern to duplicate the angle of each slope of the roof.

The two popular shingle materials are wood and asphalt. Wood is probably the most widely used because it is included in so many of the tab-and-slot and tongue-and-groove houses. Usually, the wood comes as individual pieces and the asphalt is a continuous roll. The cottage sample in this book is a little unusual in that the wood shingles came as a sheet and each row had to be cut out. The shingles were not distinctly marked, which gave the roof a sharp horizontal delineation. The texture of the wood makes one think of thatching, although in reality it isn't. The only difference in installing the two roofing materials is the wood is glued on and the asphalt is stapled in place.

Use Tacky glue with the wood, or a lightweight staple gun and ¼" staples for the asphalt. A desk stapler will do if it opens flat. Tape the row of asphalt shingles in place, so both hands are free to operate the stapler. Remove the tape before doing the next row.

WOODEN SHINGLES

I left the wooden shingles in the book their natural color, but you may want to stain them a different color either before or after installation. If you want to use an oil-base stain, it is probably easier to coat them before installation. Pour the stain into a bowl and add the shingles a few at a time. As you remove them, wipe them off and lay them out to dry.

The other way to stain the shingles is to install them first. Be careful not to get glue on the surface of the shingles—it becomes a white spot that is difficult to cover, especially with oil-base stain.

Most of the time when shingles are stained after installation, it is to make them look weathered. You use acrylic paint for this. Burnt umber, black, and green are some of the colors used to give the shingles the look of age, mold, mildew, and moss.

Since you will probably want deeper color at the top edge of the shingles, you can make gravity help you by laying your house on its back before applying the stain or wash. The thin color will then pool toward the top of the shingles. Protect the rest of the house by covering the finished parts while you work.

The first wash to put on the roof is a mixture of burnt umber and black. Thin the color with water and a little acrylic extender. (This comes in a bottle and adds moisture to the paint without loss of color intensity.) Apply a thin coat and let it dry. If it's not as dark as you would like, apply a second coat. Experiment on a sample section of roofing to see how the paint wash will move.

If you want the roof to look mossy, add some darkened green to the edges of some of the shingles. Use a thicker mix of color and water and a light touch. Any foliage green you like, or that works with your color scheme, may be darkened a bit with black. Apply the black-green by stippling with a lightly loaded brush or small piece of sponge. Just add the moss randomly to areas of the roof that could conceivably stay damp, like valleys and eaves. Don't cover the whole roof as you did with the first wash.

Another reason to stain the roof is to change its color to match the scheme of the house. For example, an Easter house can be done with a yellow shell, pink shutters, light blue door, and a violet roof. Thinning the violet paint for the wash on the roof softens the color so the whole has a cheery springtime look. No matter how you color the roof, don't finish with a shiny varnish—leave it natural.

The best way to apply wooden shingles is to attach them with Tacky glue. The glue sets slowly enough that you can usually apply it to the whole row and get all the shingles in place before it dries too much for the shingles to stick. There are only two places where the shingle will come in contact with the roof—along the grid line on the roof and along the top edge of the shingles in the previous row. These are the two places where you run your line of glue. Then quickly put the shingles in place, lining them up with the grid lines and following the pattern you've set up.

If you cover the entire surface on the back of a shingle with Tacky, it usually warps. Acrylic washes can also cause warping. Irregular shingles are a natural look in an aged roof. This may be an effect you want if you are doing a house showing a weathered exterior.

ASPHALT SHINGLES

These shingles come in a roll, 1 or 3 square feet to the box. I recommend applying them with a staple gun and 1/4" staples. This method works well on roofs that are 1/4" thick or more. On 1/8" plywood roofs, however, glue the shingles in place, because 1/4" staples go right through the wood. Use Quick Grab, applying it with one line of glue along the grid line and dotting the back of each shingle on a line between the slits. You may have to use masking tape to hold the shingles down until the glue sets. Apply the glue sparingly so it doesn't ooze through the slits.

The shingle roll comes in a dispenser box. If you tear off the cardboard strap and tear out the small cardboard section of the lid, the box will dispense the shingles smoothly. It also helps to lay the box so the smooth edge of the shingle roll is down.

Work the largest roof on the dollhouse first. That way any short strips that are left at the end of a roll may be used for the smaller rows or saved for the roof ridge.

Lay a half-width row of shingles first. Measure one length of shingles to fit the bottom edge of the roof. Trim the shingles off, leaving a 1/2" strip of roofing. Apply this to the bottom edge of the roof, barely overhanging the edge—about the width of a

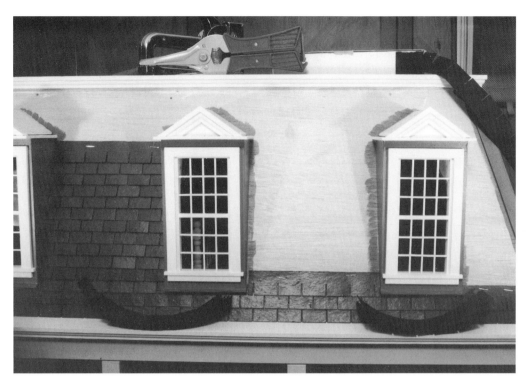

The box of shingles on top of the house lies so the straight edge of the shingle strip is fed smoothly out of the box.

scissors blade. I recommend a narrow overhang to prevent damage to the roofing when you use the house.

To determine where you can put the staples in the starter row, have the first full row measured out and taped above it. Put your staples in the area that will be underneath the shingles in the next row. On subsequent rows, apply the staples above the slits in the shingle pattern.

To measure out the first roll, pull out a length of shingles and hold it against the dollhouse roof. Center it so the middle shingle is centered over the center line on the roof and there is a partial shingle or one shingle hanging off the end. Trim the end at the box the same way. This is the pattern for the odd rows. Measure the next, or even, row the same way, except that a slit falls on the center line of the roof. Measure and cut five or six pieces of each row. Then go to the dollhouse and attach them to the roof.

The best cutting tool for the shingles seems to be a Snips or similar kitchen scissors. As you apply each row, trim the ends to cover the edge but not so much that they can be easily caught and damaged. Again, the width of the Snips blade seems to be a good allowance.

If you have roof valleys, make an angle duplicator, as described under wooden shin-

gles. Use this guide to trim the angles on each row. Cover all the roof area and apply the roof ridge.

FINISH THE ROOF RIDGE

I supplied a description of various roof ridge finishes in Chapter 7. Here are the instructions for installing them.

FOLDED SHINGLE RIDGE

This is the most realistic ridge finish. It is used on the Twelve Oaks roof. I cut individual shingles from the roll scraps, folded each shingle lengthwise and attached them to the roof with staples, one on each side of the peak. I overlapped the shingles about ¼", covering the patterned edge of the shingle.

When you have a roof or part of the roof running into the house, always start the ridge row against the house

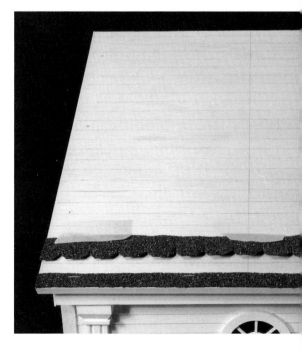

Attaching the bottom half-width starter roll of shingles.

The folded asphalt shingle ridge trim.

A dowel and strip- wood ridge finish.

they give a rounded, almost molded look.

DOWEL AND STRIPWOOD RIDGE

I used this ridge on the Heritage. That roof has a steep pitch, so when I folded the wooden shingles to cover the ridge, they cracked. They also were very chunky looking. I decided to use a dowel and stripwood instead. For a realistic look I could have painted the ridge trim a metal color. Most metal roof trim turns to a dull gray. However, the Heritage is in part a fantasy house, so I stained the roof ridges with Early American stain, which is close to the redwood of the shingles.

and work away from it. That way the shingle slants away from the house, causing the rainwater to run off.

I finished the roof on the Glencroft with folded shingles also, gluing and taping them in place. They didn't crack when applied, so

After I stained the wood, I cut it to fit the house peaks. I finished the ridge on one of the secondary roofs with only a dowel. The interlock of the shingles at that outside corner wasn't smooth, the folded shingles were

too thick, and I simply felt the dowel was a nicer finish.

Another option I had along that ridge would have been to interlock the shingles. The first row would have the ridge shingle on one side long enough to cover the edge of the shingle on the other. This edge would be finished to the contour of the row. On the second row, I would have reversed the procedure so that the opposite side was covered. In this arrangement the shingle seam alternates up the ridge. This type of inter-locking should only be done on steeply sloping peaks or on the side of a house if it has a shingle finish.

DECORATIVE SHINGLE RIDGE

To create the illusion of a thatched roof, I cut the top row of shingles on the Glencroft in a decorative pattern. The first two shin-gles in a row formed the scallop and the third shingle was cut in a V shape. I cut the pattern with a pair of scissors. Then I fin-ished the peak with a folded shingle ridge.

A decorative edge was cut into the top row of shingles. The ridge was covered with folded shinges.

17 INSTALLING STAIRCASES

The partially assembled staircase for the Heritage is ready to be slid into place and finished.

The spacing jig used for the second-floor bannister in the Heritage.

The last part to add to the dollhouse is the staircase. At this point you should have the staircase room fully decorated, with only the moldings and staircase to be added. By now you have probably at least read about how the stairs fit into the house and maybe even have tack-glued it together to understand the mechanics of getting it in the house.

Gather all the parts to the staircase together with the instructions. Identify the pieces according to your kit description and do a trial run constructing the staircase. Tape it together or carefully tack-glue it. Make sure the parts fit, with the holes for spindles the right size and the spacers in the right place.

Don't expect staircases to fit perfectly. I had to do some finagling on all the sample houses to get them fitted right.

I did the construction of the Heritage in a different order from that of the other houses. As shown in the photo on the previous page, this was as far I could build it before putting the stairs in the house.

The treads and landing had holes in them to seat the spindles in. I had to cut the handrail to fit, and this really couldn't be done until the staircase was in the house. The spindles on the upper staircase look askew because they had to give a little to get the stairs in place. Once the stairs were there, I straightened the spindles and installed the handrail, anchoring the spindles, since it was also glued to the railing on the floor above.

The spindles of the bannister on the second floor around the stairwell were supposed to seat into pre-drilled holes in the floor. Since there was some extra small edge trim, I constructed the bannister with the trim top and bottom and then glued it in place.

I made a spacing jig with scrap wood (see above). Since the spindles were $1/8$" in diameter, I glued scrap $3/8$" wood to a base with a $1/8$" space. This made a perfect $1/2$" spaced bannister, matching the rest of the staircase.

In the Glencroft, I trimmed each stair tread $1/8$" along the nosing, since it was much too wide to go under carpeting. In the Twelve Oaks I added an extra newel post. These are just a few examples of things to look for that can make your house a little more polished.

Decide how you will finish your stairs. Generally, it's best to do it while it's in pieces. Stain, paint, and finish as much as possible before you glue it together.

A general guideline for finishing the stairs is to stain the treads and handrails the same

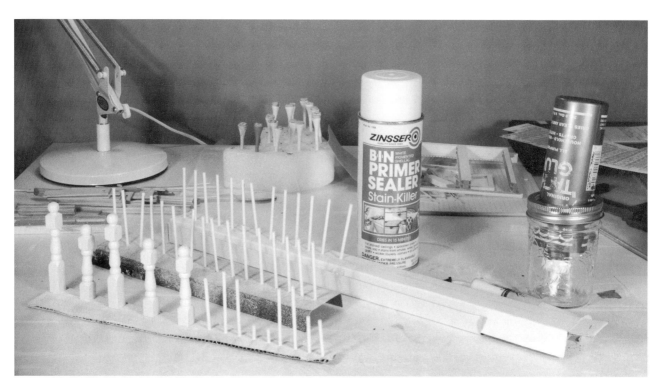

Like the other woodwork in a house, the parts of a staircase need careful finishing.

color as the wooden floors, and paint the risers, spindles, and newel post the same color as the woodwork trim. The newel post may also be stained instead of painted. Using that rule, it's easy to see how the color scheme came about for the Twelve Oaks—a house with white woodwork and fruitwood floors. If you were working on a house with stained woodwork and stained floors, a fully stained staircase would be appropriate.

In the Heritage, the staircase ended up all stained oak except for the white stair stringer (the side framing that holds the risers and steps). I did it this way so the staircase blended into the decorations.

Sort the stair parts so all the pieces to be stained are in one stack and the pieces to be painted are in another. Make holding jigs from cardboard and glue the stair pieces to them, still keeping the pieces to be stained separate from those to be painted. Run a line of Tacky glue down the middle of the cardboard. Stand the newel posts and spindles upright in the glue. Space them far enough apart so you can spray-paint them or paint them by brush.

Treat separate stair treads similarly. Glue the wrong side of them to a piece of cardboard. If separate, the stair risers should be on a separate cardboard, since they usually are painted. Often the stair risers are solid and already assembled as the base unit for the staircase. Finish the risers, the open side of the staircase, and its back at the same time. Usually you can lay this unit on the side that will remain unfinished, so it can easily be painted.

Prime all the parts to be painted with spray white-pigmented shellac. When the parts are dry, rub them down with a brown paper bag and paint them. I used brush-on paint on the examples in this book in order to control runs.

For the parts to be stained, I applied color with a brush and wiped the excess off with a soft dry rag. A coat of clear shellac set up the surface. When dry I rubbed it down with the paper bag and applied final coats of water-base varnish. On some woods you'll only need only one coat of varnish after using the clear shellac.

Assemble the staircases according to the directions in your kit. Set them in the house temporarily so you can measure and cut the remaining room moldings. At the back, slanted side of the staircase, mark along its edge on the wall. Remove the stairs and fit and cut the moldings that go there and install them.

Glue the stairs permanently in place. Now, fit, cut, and install the moldings that go in front of the stairs.

Turn on the lights in your dollhouse. Check every room to be sure you have installed every light and all the trim. See that everything is glued in place. Use filler and touch up with paint where necessary. And, yes—the house is finished! Enjoy each splendid corner! And don't forget to put the finish date into your planning journal.

The finished staircases in the Twelve Oaks.

18 DOLLHOUSE DISPLAY

Bring your newly finished dollhouse out of the workroom and put it on display in an area where you can see it several times a day. Share it with your friends. Even if this is a house to go to grandchildren, enjoy it before you give it away. Even if you've made the house for your child, still display it where you can show it off.

Adult miniature collectors think of ingenious places to show off their dollhouses—

The Twelve Oaks is displayed on a table with casters.

living rooms, family rooms, kitchens, and dining rooms, and sometimes a spare bedroom that is the Dollhouse Room. It's fun to incorporate the dollhouse into your other furnishings. Any niche has possibilities.

Children love having their dollhouses in their rooms where they can take their friends to play. Most of the time their houses seem to end up living on the floor so they can see in the top level. If possible, it's best to place the house on a table the height of a child's table. Sturdy TV stands are a good choice for holding a child's dollhouse. Then the children don't have to crawl around on their tummies to see in the lowest level.

The most popular stand to hold the house is a sturdy table, like an occasional table, conference table, or flat-top trunk. The houses in this book will have varied resting places. The Newport will sit on a trunk in the living room. The Heritage will be displayed on a gate-leg table at Christmas, probably in lieu of a Christmas tree. The Twelve Oaks will have its own conference table in the workroom. The Glencroft will rest on a square oak parlor table.

The conference table used for the Twelve Oaks was customized

for the house. It has a solid top and folding legs and measures 30" x 72". It's available at our local office supply superstore.

This table has metal tube legs fitted with plastic caps. I popped the caps off the legs and replaced them with plastic caster holders and metal casters. This makes an easily moved table that allows access to the front and back of the house. The table is reasonably priced, and it's only 30 minutes of work to remove the caps and install the rollers. The convenience of the moveable table is an ongoing delight.

Most dollhouse owners keep the landscaping to a minimum around their houses. If they want outbuildings or a garden they usually make it a separate project. The examples in this book have been treated this way. Two houses were set on bases and the other three are simply set on the table.

Make landscaping as permanent as possible. For this reason artificial imitations of foliage are preferable. Painted grass and snow, "bottle brush" evergreens, and metal and foam trees will last a long time. Paper and fabric products are usable, although it's necessary to keep them out of strong light, as they tend to fade. Dried plant products are beautiful but have a limited life expectancy.

The simplest setting for the dollhouse is a tabletop painted green. A collector from England created a lovely one with fancy routed edges that were as beautifully finished as a fine piece of furniture.

My grandfather put a green tabletop on a toy cabinet he made just to hold my one-story house. The dollhouse was just the right level. My sister and I could stand and play in it, or we could drag a chair to it and sit at the house. The tabletop had a deep overhang above the cabinet underneath. This piece of furniture was on casters.

The largest of the sample houses, the Twelve Oaks, is on a green felt tablecloth on

The window box is filled with colorful silk flowers and foam foliage.

the movable table. No further landscaping is planned for now, but if I add something later it will be a movable unit that I can change for different seasons of the year. I will treat the Newport the same way. With its front-opening wall, any landscaping would have to be removable.

Both the Glencroft and Heritage rest on separate bases. I did this because they are on turntables and their foundations are not solid. The base presents a full connection with the turntable board.

I cut the base under the Glencroft from ¼" plywood. I determined the width of the base by changing the house fencing. What were meant to be side pieces became part of the front fencing. The depth accommodates the house and the front garden. I stained and finished ½" quarter-round and used it to edge the plywood base. The grass is a paper-backed fiber product made by Busch. A similar product made by Noch is available through your local miniature shop. The stone courtyard is the same Magic Ston I used on the chimney and fireplaces. The flowers in the window box are silk with foam

foliage. Eventually the house will be covered with roses and clematis and the gardens with cottage flowers.

Short-pile artificial grass carpeting is usable as grass too. It's very permanent. To make it appear in scale, you must frame it with molding to hide the depth of the pile. This could have been used for the Glencroft because the quarter-round edging was deep enough to hide the grass depth.

I made the base for the Heritage from 1" thick particle board. The size for this house was measured from the bays and the protruding downspouts, plus an inch. The front-to-back measurement was only increased by a couple of inches. This is a winter house, so snow is permanently on the ground. I planted a few evergreens to break up the large amounts of brick foundation. The evergreens are bottle brush trees with a wood product foliage. I drilled holes in the base for the wire tree trunks and glued them in place with Tacky. Then I finished the edges of the base with the snow. To have the snow go over the edge of the board gives the impression of depth.

Pieces of green foliage lie on the sparkling snow base.

The snow on this base is a textured paint called Snow-Tex. To further enhance it, I painted a coat of Sparkle Glaze over it. This has very fine iridescent glitter in it. It's a pleasing finish, as the glitter appears in scale and so the snow sparkles in the sunshine.

"Sandstones" is a textured paint that imitates a cement sidewalk. There are many new textured paints at the craft store. It's worth a browse to see what new finishes you may find.

The Cranberry Cove, meant to be played with, is built with the floor on the first level as the base. This is solid as is, so the house needs no further support. Felt feet raise it just a little off the table surface to protect the bottom edges of the siding.

These examples should give you some ideas for setting up your dollhouse display. Move your dollhouse to its special nook and begin filling it with all the wonderful miniature furnishings you've been collecting. It's time to bring those things out of the closet and shoe boxes and into your dollhouse.

Now it can truly be said your dollhouse is finished . . . until you start the next one!

APPENDIX A

KEY TO SUPPLIES USED IN THE DOLLHOUSES

CRANBERRY COVE

Hardware: Houseworks.
Kit: Walmer Dollhouses. Kit includes doors, windows, and staircases.
Lighting: Cir-kit Concepts, Miniature House.
Moldings: Midwest.
Paint: Builder's Choice, Ceramacoat, Min-Wax.
Siding: Midwest.
Wallpaper: MiniGraphics. Applied with MiniGraphics Mucilage.

GLENCROFT

Carpeting: B.H. Miniatures.
Hardware: Houseworks, Realife.
Kit: Greenleaf Products. Kit includes doors and windows, interior doors, some moldings, shingles, and staircase.
Landscaping: Miniature Corner.
Lighting: Electalite, Miniature House.
Moldings: Midwest.
Paint: Builder's Choice, Min-Wax.
Stone: Magic Systems.
Tile: J.R. Enterprises.
Wallpaper: B.H. Miniatures, MiniGraphics. Applied with cellulose wallpaper paste.

HERITAGE

Hardware: Houseworks, Clare-Bell Brass.

Kit: Dura-craft. Kit includes brick, doors and windows, moldings, shingles, siding, staircases, and wooden flooring.

Landscaping: New England Hobby Supply, Delta Paint.

Lighting: Cir-Kit Concepts.

Paint: Builder's Choice.

Wallpaper: J. Hermes Miniatures. Applied with Grandma Stover's Stickflat Glue.

NEWPORT

Brick: Magic Systems.

Doors and Windows: Timberbrook.

Fireplaces: Braxton Payne, Houseworks.

Hardware: Realife, VIX Miniatures, Clare-Bell Brass.

Interior Doors: Timberbrook.

Kit: Afton Classics. Kit includes exterior door, windows, and staircases.

Lighting: Clare-Bell Brass, Cir-Kit Concepts.

Moldings: Northeastern, Midwest.

Paint: Builder's Choice.

Shingles: What's Next.

Staircases: Timberbrook.

Tile: Eden Craft.

Wallpaper: B.H. Miniatures, Tiny-Tiques. Applied with Builder's Choice Wallpaper Gel.

Wooden Flooring: Handley House.

TWELVE OAKS

Brick: Real Good Toys.

Carpeting: Minigraphics.

Doors and Windows: Houseworks.

Hardware: Houseworks, Realife.

Interior Doors: Houseworks.

Kit: Real Good Toys. Kit includes brick, exterior doors and
windows, siding, and staircases.

Lighting: The Happy Unicorn, Scott's Lighting, Miniature House,
Cir-Kit Concepts.

Moldings: Northeastern, Midwest, Houseworks.

Mullions: New England Hobby.

Paint: Builder's Choice.

Shingles: What's Next.

Siding: Northeastern.

Tile: J.R. Enterprises.

Wallpaper: Minigraphics.

Wooden Flooring: Midwest.

APPENDIX B

MANUFACTURERS AND SUPPLIERS

Most of the companies listed below are manufacturers and sell merchandise whole-sale only to retail shops and mail order companies. If you are interested in purchasing their products, ask for them at your local miniature shop or through your favorite mail order catalog. You may give the shop the company's name and address from this list. If a supplier is a retailer, that will be noted under the company listing.

AFTON CLASSICS
   37 COMMERCE ST.
   CHATHAM, NJ 07928
   Newport dollhouse kit.

B.H. MINIATURES
   20805 N. 19TH AVE. #5
   PHOENIX, AZ 85027
   Wallpaper and velvet carpeting.

BRAXTON PAYNE MINIATURES
   P. O. BOX 54431
   ATLANTA, GA 30308
   Fireplaces. Sells retail too.

CIR-KIT CONCEPTS, INC.
   407 14TH ST. NW
   ROCHESTER, MN 55901
   Tape wire electrical systems and Miniature House lighting.

CLARE-BELL BRASS WORKS
   P. O. BOX 218
   LOVELL, ME 04051
   Lighting fixtures, weather vanes, and house numbers.

DEE'S DELIGHTS, INC.
   3150 STATE LINE RD.
   NORTH BEND, OH 45052-9731
   Magic Systems Brik and Ston, Eden's Craft slate tile.

DURA-CRAFT, INC.
   P. O. BOX 438
   NEWBERG, OR 97132
   Heritage dollhouse kit.

GREENLEAF PRODUCTS, INC.
   58 N. MAIN
   P. O. BOX 388
   HONEYOYE FALLS, NY 14472
   Glencroft dollhouse kit, Electalite tape wire and light fixtures.

HANDLEY HOUSE
   2 FOURTH ST.
   WHEELING, WV 26003
   Wooden flooring, Miniature House flooring and light fixtures.

THE HAPPY UNICORN
   901 ELLYNWOOD DR.
   GLEN ELLYN, IL 60137
   Crystal chandeliers. Also sells retail.

HOUSEWORKS, LTD.
   2388 PLEASANTDALE RD.
   ATLANTA, GA 30340
   Doors and windows, interior doors, hardware, moldings.

J. HERMES MINIATURES
   9606 LAS TUNAS DR.
   TEMPLE CITY, CA 91780
   Wallpaper. Also sells retail.

J.R. ENTERPRISES
    53 CASE RD.
    PORT JERVIS, NY 12771-9442
    Embossed plastic sheet tile.

MIDWEST PRODUCTS, INC.
    400 S. INDIANA ST.
    P.O. BOX 564
    HOBART, IN 46342
    Clapboard siding, flooring, moldings,
    stripwood.

MINIGRAPHICS
    2975 EXON AVE.
    CINCINNATI, OH 45241
    Wallpaper and velvet carpeting.

MINIATURE CORNER, INC.
    303 CLAY AVE.
    JEANETTE, PA 15644
    Noch landscaping grass.

NEW ENGLAND HOBBY SUPPLY
    71 HILLIARD ST.
    MANCHESTER, CT 06040-3001
    Builder's Choice paint and wallpaper
    gel, bushes for landscaping, mullions.

NORTHEASTERN SCALE MODELS,
    INC.
    99 CROSS ST.
    P. O. BOX 727
    METHUEN, MA 01844
    Moldings, siding, stripwood.

REAL GOOD TOYS
    10 QUARRY HILL
    BARRE, VT 05641
    Twelve Oaks dollhouse kit, wooden
    brick strips.

SCOTT'S LIGHTING
    HC 60 BOX 29BB
    CABLE, WI 54821
    Brass coachlights. Retail sales only.

TIMBERBROOK WOOD PRODUCTS
    HOVEY LN.
    SOUTH NEW BERLIN, NY 13843
    Doors and windows, interior doors,
    staircases.

TINY TIQUES
    P. O. BOX 957251
    HOFFMAN ESTATES, IL 60195-7251
    Wallpaper. Retail shows only. No mail
    order.

WALMER DOLLHOUSES
    2100 JEFFERSON DAVIS HWY.
    ALEXANDRIA, VA 22301-3102
    Cranberry Cove dollhouse kit.

WHAT'S NEXT?
    1000 CEDAR AVE.
    SCRANTON, PA 18505
    Asphalt shingles.

INDEX